DOCTOR of HOPE

OKLAHOMA *TRACKMAKER* SERIES

BOB FUNK

Doctor of Hope

by **BOB BURKE** *and* **DAVE GILLOGLY**

Series Editor: Gini Moore Campbell
Associate Editor: Eric Dabney

FOREWORD BY DR. LLOYD OGILVIE

OKLAHOMA
HERITAGE
ASSOCIATION
Oklahoma City

Printed in the United States of America by Jostens, Inc.
ISBN 10: 1-885596-54-5
ISBN 13: 978-1-885596-54-3
Library of Congress Catalog Number 2007926372
Designed by Sandi Welch/2WDesignGroup.com
Cover photo by Robert Burke

Unless otherwise noted, photographs are courtesy of Bob and Nedra Funk or Express Personnel Services.

Contents

ACKNOWLEDGMENTS   5
FOREWORD by Dr. Lloyd Ogilvie   7

one A DEFINING MOMENT   11
two HARD TIMES IN KING COUNTY   15
three LEARNING ABOUT HARD WORK   37
four OFF TO COLLEGE   53
five EDINBURGH   61
six A COLD SCOTTISH WINTER   71
seven A CHANGE IN DIRECTION   79
eight INSIDE WORK   87
nine MY KIND OF COUNTRY   99
ten OUT OF THE ASHES   117
eleven THRIVING AGAIN   131
twelve CRITICAL TIMES   145
thirteen A JOB FOR EVERY PERSON AND A PERSON FOR EVERY JOB   155
fourteen STRENGTH FOR THE FUTURE   169
fifteen BOB—THE COWBOY   181
sixteen PUCKS AND LOBS   197
seventeen SULTAN OF SPORTS   213
eighteen PUBLIC SERVICE   221
nineteen GIVING HOPE   237
THE NEXT TO THE LAST CHAPTER   245

NOTES   247
INDEX   253

PAY TO THE ORDER OF *Acme Personnel Service of Spokane, Inc.* 22-21 19 82   86-209 / 1031

Thirty-Eight Thousand Nine Hundred Sixty and 33/100 DOLLARS $38,960.33

Rolling Hills STATE BANK
P.O. BOX 58 • PIEDMONT, OKLAHOMA 73078

For *Down Payment of Acme - OKC*   *Robert G. Funk*

Acknowledgments

It was an exciting task to trace the footsteps of Bob and Nedra Funk. We could not have done so without the help of many people, including Bob and Nedra, who willingly gave their time for extensive interviews and rummaging through boxes of photographs and mementos.

Bob's sister, Joanne Benton, provided a wealth of knowledge and priceless photographs of Bob's early life. Linda Haneborg at Express Personnel guided us through the maze of information and coordinated the entire project. We are grateful to Sean Simpson, Tiffany Monhollon, Summer Short, Jennifer Kenley, and Marisa Quinn for their editorial assistance.

Thanks to our editors, Gini Moore Campbell and Eric Dabney, and proofreaders George and Marcia Davis, Judge Mary Black, and Judge Cheri Farrar. Linda Lynn, Mary Phillips, Melissa Hayer, Robin Davison, and Billie Harry at the archives of *The Oklahoman* provided photographs and information. Debbie Neill and Michelle Douglas transcribed the interviews of many people who provided details of Bob's exciting journey. Sandi Welch did her usual magnificent job in designing the book.

We are grateful to the Oklahoma Heritage Association, its president, Shannon Nance, director of publications, Gini Moore Campbell, and chairman, Glen D. Johnson, Jr., for a continuing commitment to preserve the story of Oklahoma.

—Bob Burke
Dave Gillogly
2007

Foreword

WHAT WILLIAM PENN SAID of George Fox could well be said of Bob Funk; "He is an original and no man's copy."

Bob Funk is not only an original, but an originator, an instigator, an enabler, and a visionary. He is a truly great man filled with faith in God, a profound love for people, and a passion to help them succeed.

Whenever I think of Bob Funk, I picture his broad smile, his eyes that twinkle with enthusiasm for life, his keen interest in people, and his affirmation of potential in every person he meets.

Bob stands tall both physically and ethically, he stands firm with integrity and intentionality, and he strides forward with one goal—bettering people's lives. "Life is all about people," Bob says.

You are about to read a book about this remarkable man. He is one of the most successful men in our time.

It is a stimulating, compelling biography of a distinguished businessman, and it is a motivational page-turner with clearly illustrated principles of dynamic leadership.

In this book, you will meet a man who epitomizes the American dream of the opportunity to rise from a very modest, humble background to the heights of professional and personal achievement.

Here's a read that will move you to a fresh commitment to excellence, encourage you to risk in order to accomplish your goals, help you decide never to give up even when circumstances are discouraging, and assure you again that hard work and indefatigable courage have not gone out of style.

As Bob Funk himself puts it, "The key is to do what's right and charge down the road."

The title of this book, *Bob Funk: Doctor of Hope,* is spot-on. Bob has diagnosed the fundamental need in people to find truly satisfying employment and developed a powerful prescription with Express Services, Inc., whose methods and principles of helping people find satisfying and fulfilling work are truly inspired.

He has made his life's business inspiring hope in people who need a job. Bob exudes hope in his positive approach to life.

The bedrock foundation for Bob Funk's hope comes from his relationship with God. Because Bob believes in Him as the Lord of the impossible, nothing seems impossible to attempt. What God guides, He provides.

The greatness of Bob Funk is expressed in his irrepressible gratitude which is the motivation of his immense generosity. He and his beloved wife, Nedra, have expressed an attitude of gratitude in giving millions of dollars to strategic causes and projects in Oklahoma, throughout our nation, and to urgent needs in the world. The Funks put into practice John Wesley's admonition, "Earn all you can, save all you can, and give all you can."

You will enjoy this book. It will make you glad that you're an American and will reaffirm that free enterprise does work, that people count, and that you too can be a communicator of hope to those around you.

—LLOYD JOHN OGILVIE
Former Chaplain,
United States Senate

American Broadcasting Company

Young North Carolina Baptist evangelist Billy Graham came to Seattle, Washington, in 1951 to hold one of his first city-wide crusades. *Courtesy Billy Graham Evangelistic Association.*

One

A DEFINING MOMENT

THE LAST RAYS OF THE SUMMER SUN slid behind the rim of the football stadium on a pleasant evening in July, 1951, in Seattle, Washington. Eleven-year-old Bob Funk and several of his cousins and friends from the Methodist Church in his tiny hometown of Duvall had traveled by bus to attend the opening night of an evangelistic crusade led by Billy Graham, a young North Carolina Baptist preacher.

Bob's group sat in folding chairs on the grass football field of Taft Stadium about 30 rows back from the stage where Reverend Graham, musicians, and ministers from the Seattle area sat.

There had been special singing by George Beverly Shea, a deep-voiced soloist whose mellow notes rang out majestically in the Seattle night air. After leaders of the community were introduced, Reverend Graham began telling the story of how a personal relationship with Christ had changed the direction of his life. Bob sat reverently as Reverend Graham delivered a simple sermon of salvation by accepting Jesus Christ as a personal savior.

The need for salvation was not a novel concept to Bob. He knew a lot about Christ—he rarely missed Sunday School and church services at the Duvall Methodist Church. He knew from memory the lessons he had heard at church and home about the death and resurrection of Christ. But until that moment, it had been only a story about a great man.

Toward the end of Reverend Graham's sermon, Bob felt a tugging at his heart. He was strongly convinced that he was a sinner. A heaviness set upon him. Even at the tender age of 11, he realized he needed the help of Christ to rescue him. He felt sure that Reverend Graham was looking only at him when the invitation was given to the huge crowd that packed the field and the stadium seats.

Reverend Graham's words were simple and straightforward, "This is your time of decision. Tonight, you can accept Jesus Christ as your Savior, and your life will never be the same." Bob's mind raced as he wondered what to do. Would his friends laugh at him if he decided to answer Reverend Graham's invitation and walk toward the stage to accept Christ? Was he really old enough to make this kind of momentous decision? After Reverend Graham completed his sermon, the crusade choir began singing "Just As I Am," the hymn that would become the trademark of hundreds of Billy Graham crusades around the world.

Feeling the pressure of the moment and his need for salvation, Bob sincerely believed that if he did not go forward, his rejection of Christ might cause the church bus to crash on the way home in the Snoqualmie Valley and injure or kill him along with his friends and adult leaders. The burden of his heart was great, without hesitation he stood and moved toward the stage. He did not notice that many of his cousins and friends from the Methodist youth group also had walked quickly to the stage area where they were met by counselors who gave them literature. Reverend Graham led them in a prayer for salvation.

As soon as Bob prayed for salvation, he felt a load lift. He knew he had done the right thing. A feeling of cleanliness and wholesomeness filled his mind and body. He did not yet know the depth of his decision, but the months and years ahead would define his commitment to God. He would develop a burning desire to go in three separate directions in his life, all at the same time to become a preacher, a farmer, and a businessman. He did not know how his dreams would be accomplished, but he placed his faith in God to make them happen.

The 1951 Billy Graham Crusade in Seattle was important to both the evangelist and to Bob Funk. It was one of the first city-wide crusades held by Graham, who would become the best known Christian evangelist in the twentieth century and confidant of every President of the United States during his ministry. Bob's decision, one of more than 6,000 reported decisions for Christ in the six-week crusade, would impact his life in an unbelievable way and guide him on a journey that would ultimately lead him to Oklahoma and a position as one of the nation's most successful and respected business leaders.

Bob's father, seated, and his three sisters, left to right, Ruth, Elnora, and Alta Funk.

Two

HARD TIMES IN KING COUNTY

THE STORY OF ROBERT ALLEN "BOB" FUNK began in the early part of the twentieth century when his grandmother emigrated from Poznan, Germany, to Indiana, then to the tiny town of Duvall, Washington, on the banks of the Snoqualmie River.

Duvall, a village of 300 hard-working people, was a hillside homesteaded by James and Francis Duvall in the 1870s. The town's namesake was a logger, felling huge trees that grew in the foothills of the Cascade Range, a mountain chain that runs north-south along the west coast of North America from British Columbia to northern California. The forests on the slopes east of the Snoqualmie River were rich with Douglas fir, Western Hemlock, and Western Red Cedar. Trees were felled and transported down the river to the Puget Sound, an arm of the Pacific Ocean.[1]

Logging brought the railroad and a logging camp called Cherry Valley. In 1909, the Chicago, Milwaukee, and St. Paul Railroad built a line across the river for better access to the forests. The town of Cherry Valley was in the way of the railroad, so the town was moved. After a brief time bearing the name of Cosgrove, the town was renamed Duvall and incorporated in 1913.[2]

By the time the Funks arrived in King County, named for William Rufus King, vice president under President of the United

Bob's grandmother, Pearl Addleman Funk, and her father, James Franklin Addelman, participated in the Alaska Gold Rush. Her mother was Emma Katherine Addleman.

States Franklin Pierce, Duvall was a sharp contrast to the county's most famous city, Seattle, 20 miles to the west. Early in Washington's history, Seattle became the county seat of King County and quickly became the most populous city in the state.[3]

While Seattle had wide, paved streets, Duvall's streets were dirt and full of ruts that were a testament to the time when loggers pulled huge logs down the streets before dumping them in the river to float toward a mill in Everett, Washington.

The logging industry had diminished in importance in the Snoqualmie Valley when the Funks made their home in Duvall. Instead of lumber products, dairy farms became the focus of the region's economy. The world-famous Carnation Dairy operation was established in 1910 about ten miles from Duvall in the rural community of Tolt. The town later was renamed Carnation, although old timers still referred to the village as Tolt, partly because the name had been in use for generations, a derivation of "Tolthue," the Snoqualmie name for "river of swift water." There is still confusion over what the town should be called—some maps show both names.[4]

The cleared prairie was very suitable for dairy farming. After Elbridge Amos Stuart cleared 350 acres of timber and brush and brought in a purebred bull and 86 registered Holstein cows to build the first Carnation Dairy, the valley became known as the "Home for Contented Cows."[5]

Bob's grandfather, William Allen Funk, was a King County homesteader in the late years of the nineteenth century. Born in Nebraska, he settled with his wife, Pearl Francis Addleman Funk, in Duvall and began working in the logwoods until it became economically more practical to raise dairy cattle and produce milk.[6]

Bob's father, Allen Roy Funk, was born in August, 1907, in Duvall. As a youngster, he began milking cows and helping his father on the dairy farm where 25 Jersey cows grazed on 40 acres. To earn additional money for the family, Roy—he was generally known by his middle name—took jobs hand-milking cows on various dairies around Duvall. It was such hard work that it was not unusual for Roy to require his right arm to be massaged when he returned home at night.[7]

As the Great Depression gripped the area in the 1930s, Roy milked as many as 30 cows three times a day. It was extremely hard work, but the pay kept the family alive. Roy did not have many options as far as employment was concerned. He had dropped out of school in the eighth grade to help supplement the family income.[8]

As Roy approached his adult years, he fell in love with Dorothy Ellen Herman, who had moved from her native Indiana home with her mother, Emma Marie Herman, to the Snoqualmie Valley in 1922 at the age of 13. Emma Marie was trying to escape the reach of an abusive, alcoholic husband in Indiana. Dorothy's father, Julius Carl Herman, had a pattern of spending his paycheck on liquor and abusing his wife when he came home drunk.

For a new life, Emma Marie and her children were invited to live on a dairy farm with her sister, Anna Pauline, and her husband, Frank Emil Hanisch. The Hanisches had established a successful dairy operation and provided work for Emma Marie and her older children.[9]

Dorothy, called "Dot" by her family, was two years younger than Roy and tried to further her education by attending the University of Puget Sound for two years. She had graduated from high school at age 16 and earned money as a nanny for a well-to-do-family in Tacoma, Washington. Coincidentally, one of the children she cared for was Gordon Blair, for whom the most prestigious award in Express Personnel Services was later named.[10]

Roy and Dorothy were married in 1929. Roy continued to milk cows for Carnation Farms at its various locations, including Lower Carnation, located just outside Duvall. Dorothy went to work for Stapleton's grocery store in Duvall. She earned $25 a month, a fine salary that produced the bulk of the household

RIGHT: Anna Pauline Hanisch, left, and Emma Marie Herman were two of thirteen Frehauf children born in Poznan, Germany, a town that is now in Poland. In 1887, the two sisters emigrated to the United States aboard the USS *President Cleveland*. Emma was Dorothy Herman Funk's mother.

Emma Marie Herman
and four of her children,
left to right, Mae, Albert,
Art, Amelia, Dorothy,
and Emma Marie.

LEFT: Frank Emil Hanisch
settled in the Snoqualmie
Valley in the final years of the
nineteenth century.

ABOVE: Bob's uncle, Albert Herman, drove a milk truck in Seattle.

LEFT: Dorothy Herman in 1929 shortly before her marriage to Roy Funk.

income for her husband and her brother, Arthur, who lived with them.[11]

Roy's arm continued to ache so badly that Dorothy packed it with ice between milkings. Carnation was trying to establish a world record for milk production with Holstein cows, so the pressure was intense to pull every ounce of milk from the cows each day.[12]

As they began planning a family, Roy and Dorothy rented a house on the property that had been his grandfather's farm. When Roy could not find work, he kept house and prepared the family meals. With Dorothy working a full shift at the grocery store, Roy believed he should assume some of the household responsibilities.

Roy established his own small dairy herd of Jersey cows on land rented from Judge Ward Roney, Duvall's richest citizen. Roy was a good manager of cows—but not a good manager of money. He gave his cattle the best hay and grain he could afford. The cattle were happy, but Roy usually lost money each year. Once, he thought he could really get ahead by selling a prize Jersey bull for $2,000. He advertised in a national magazine and received an offer from a farmer in Wisconsin. But the following morning, Roy found the bull dead. He had doctored the animal with sulfur phosphate, but the medicine unexpectedly plugged the bull's urinary tract, resulting in death.[13]

In 1936, Dorothy gave birth to their first child, Mariann, who was born a blue baby, a victim of cyanotic heart disease which causes newborns to be blue in color because of the heart's inability to put

RIGHT: Roy and Dorothy Funk lived in Duvall across the street from a house later purchased by Dorothy.

BELOW: Roy Funk on his farm with his small herd of milk cows. By Roy's side is the trusted cow dog, Shep.

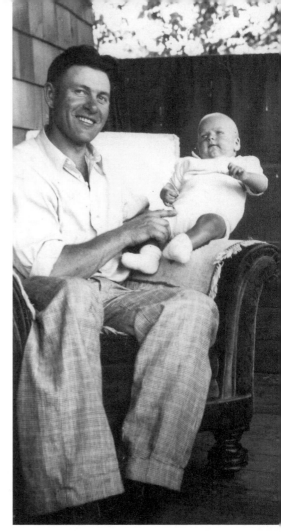

enough oxygen into the bloodstream. Because medical science had not yet developed the now commonplace method to correct the problem, the baby died three days later.[14]

On March 26, 1938, Joanne Marie Funk was born in Duvall. As with her older sister, Joanne's birth was attended by her great aunt, Ethel Michalson, a midwife who helped in the birth of many Duvall children.

Robert Allen "Bob" Funk was born on May 14, 1940, at Aunt Ethel's house, when Joanne was two years old. Shortly after Bob's birth, Dorothy had to be moved to the living room sofa because her sister-in-law, Elnora Trim, was waiting to give birth. Richard Trim was born nine days after Bob.[15]

When Bob was two, his mother suffered a nervous breakdown during a prayer meeting at church. She spent several weeks in a nearby mental hospital. However, she called her husband, complaining that her condition was getting worse because of the truly "crazy people" who were patients at the facility. Roy took Dorothy home where she remained in bed for a few years.[16]

Even though Joanne was only four years old, she was thrust into a motherly role for her baby brother. She bathed him in the kitchen sink, fed him, and changed his diapers. For several months, she and Bob were sent to live with their Grandmother Funk

RIGHT: Joanne Funk, left, assumed the role of Bob's mother during the time Dorothy Funk was suffering from the effects of a nervous breakdown.

BELOW: Dairy cows played a major role in Bob's life. On the farm, left to right, are Roy Funk, Bob, and Joanne in 1942.

because their mother was too sick to take care of them. Because the grandmother disliked Dorothy, Joanne felt an even stronger motherly instinct. "I wanted to protect Bob with all my might," she remembered, "I didn't want anything or anyone to hurt him." That motherly instinct remained with Joanne far past their childhood.[17]

When Dorothy was able to again have children around, Joanne and Bob began to visit gradually to prepare her for the atmosphere children bring to a home. On her first trip to visit her mother, Joanne cut her eye severely when she ran into a string of barbed wire that her father had recently installed across the lane to their rural home. The children were returned to their grandmother's house. When the children were able to return home permanently, Dorothy stayed in bed much of the day, but Joanne and Bob could tiptoe around and be quiet. They were glad to do so—they were happy to be home for good.

In 1945, Roy lost his lease on the acreage where he was grazing dairy cattle. He had no choice but to sell his cows and

RIGHT: Bob and his Funk cousins whose families lived in the Snoqualmie Valley of Washington. Left to right, front row, Bob, Susie Herman, Joanne Funk, and Gail Herman. Second row, Dick Herman, Nora Herman, and Carol Herman. At back is Ruth Herman.

ABOVE: Left to right, Bob, Dorothy, Roy, and Joanne Funk.

equipment and move the family into town to an 800-square-foot house on Stephens Street in Duvall. Dorothy had purchased the home from a distant cousin several years before when she was working at the grocery store. The cousin would have lost the house to the bank anyway if he did not sell it.

ABOVE: The frame house where Roy Funk moved his family in Duvall in 1945. In this 2005 photograph are, left to right, Cory Benton, Jody Strum, Bob, Joanne Benton, Terri Weldon, and Dave Benton.

RIGHT: Bob, at age four, already was helping his mother with chores around the house.

At their new home, the children slept in bunk beds on the screened-in back porch, even during the cold and wet Washington winters. Although heavy down comforters helped, Joanne and Bob often awoke cold. At first, Bob slept on the top bunk, but changed with Joanne when their mother found Bob sleepwalking off of it.[18]

This was Dorothy Funk's favorite photograph of her daughter, Joanne, at age three.

Even with Dorothy recovering from her nervous breakdown, Joanne continued to perform motherly functions. Before Bob started school, Joanne came home each day and taught him what she had learned in class that day. When Bob entered the first grade, he was far ahead of other children. When he was in the second grade, the teachers wanted him to skip a couple of grades. However, his mother declined the opportunity and kept him in the same grade with children his age.[19]

Dorothy was faithful in taking her medicine each day and grew stronger. By 1948, her physician suggested she go back to work to get her mind off the family's declining financial situation. Dorothy returned to her job at the local grocery store, although she was not paid any cash—she worked up to 65 hours each week in exchange for groceries for the family. Roy's intermittent jobs created constant hardship for the financial well-being of the family.

Finally, Roy secured a steady job. He went to work for the state highway department with the help of Bill McCormick, a local Democratic leader. Although Roy was a Republican, McCormick's influence helped him land the job with the state. Their friendship was stronger than party labels. McCormick also allowed Roy to keep four milk cows on his property one mile outside Duvall. Each morning and evening, seven days a week, Roy milked the four cows and sold the milk in 10-gallon cans to the Carnation Farms dairy. The small-scale production of milk added chores for Joanne and Bob—they churned the raw milk into butter every Saturday. The extra income made life a little easier for the Funks.[20]

From early childhood, Bob was introduced to religion by attending the Duvall Methodist Church. In fact, Dorothy began taking Bob to church when he was two weeks old, placing him in a shoe box under the back pew during the sermon. Delos

Westbrook is the first pastor he remembers. By the time Bob started school at the Cherry Valley Grade School, Dorothy had recovered from her nervous breakdown and assumed a strong role of making certain her children were in church every time the doors were open.[21]

Dorothy was a strict disciplinarian. She enforced her belief that Sunday was the day of rest. Joanne and Bob could not play baseball or any other outside games on Sundays after church. If the children were not napping, they played games together inside.[22]

The Funk children respected their mother's discipline. Dorothy would not tolerate disobedience from her children. She was not a screamer—in fact, the quieter she became, the more trouble Joanne and Bob knew they were in. They only hoped that their punishment would be a verbal reprimand. When it came time for corporal punishment, Dorothy sent the offending

BELOW: Joanne, left, and Bob Funk in May, 1942, visiting their grandfather's farm.

RIGHT: Roy Funk with Bob, left, and Joanne. Roy was hard-working, often holding down two jobs to support his family.

child to the back porch to break a switch off an imposing willow tree. Joanne received more switchings than Bob did. "Usually, he paid attention to Mama and did not disobey a second time," she remembered. "But I was the daredevil and might try to find a loophole in her instructions and make the same mistake a few days later."[23]

Joanne and Bob had normal sibling fights, although Dorothy would not allow the disagreements to escalate into sibling warfare. Once on a summer day when the two children were arguing, Dorothy made Joanne stay inside and relegated Bob to the backyard. Joanne threw a sack of garbage at Bob through an open window, forcing him to pick up the soggy items and put them in the trash can. However, the action backfired when a discarded tuna fish can hit the window sill, bounced back, and cut her finger. A neighbor had to drive her to the doctor's office for stitches.[24]

To keep Joanne and Bob from fighting while their parents were at work, Dorothy often took Bob to the grocery store with her. He passed his time stocking shelves or playing tennis on a nearby court that Dorothy could monitor from the store. Bob found a tennis racket and began taking on all opponents. Soon he became the best tennis player in Duvall.

Although discipline from their father was rare, Joanne and Bob did learn a great work ethic from him. They never heard him complain about milking cows before daylight in the winter, working eight hours for the highway department, and heading back toward the milking assignment, often after dark. As the children grew older, Dorothy worked more hours at the grocery store, often until 7:00 p.m.[25]

Dinner was always a family affair at the Funk home. Dorothy insisted that everyone eat around the table. The working parents received help on the evening meal because of a deal struck with Joanne in the eighth grade. She badly wanted an accordion, but had no money. Dorothy bought the accordion in exchange for Joanne's promise to prepare supper each night. Meals were simple. Roy wanted meat, potatoes, and vegetables, especially carrots, at major meals. The family ate so many carrots during that time they became the subject of family jokes for decades.[26]

Bob attended school from first through eighth grade at Cherry Valley Grade School, a four-room school in Duvall. Even though the building contained a basement and was two stories tall, the top floor was closed. Classes at Cherry Valley were small. There were eight students in Bob's class, five of them were his cousins.

Because a large number of the family lived in the area, the cousins spent a lot of time playing sports and getting together on weekends. Bob especially liked winter when he and his cousins and friends would navigate the steep hills of the city streets of Duvall on their sleds at 30 miles an hour. It was not unusual for winter storms to dump 12 to 14 inches of snow on Duvall.[27]

Because the school was so small, most every boy played every sport. Bob was no exception. He played on the school's basketball, softball, and soccer teams. Beginning in the fourth grade, Bob was the pitcher for the Cherry Valley softball team. There was one girl on the team from a Dutch dairy farming family that lived outside Duvall. Bob thought she was the best-looking girl in the school and had a crush on her early in his softball career.[28]

Even in his grade school years, Bob worked hard, helping his father "shock" hay in the small field where Roy grew grain for his cattle. Shocking was a less expensive method of preserving hay than baling with automated machinery. Bob raked the cut hay and piled it into windrows. When it rained—and the Snoqualmie Valley was a rainy place—the shocked hay shed raindrops to the ground. Even if the outside straw became soaked, the sunlight of the next day dried it out and the hay was saved for winter feed. Bob and Joanne also helped their parents pick strawberries in nearby fields.[29]

Bob learned to drive his father's farm truck at an early age. Even before he was tall enough to look over the steering wheel, Bob drove the red 1931 Model-A Ford truck with a dump bed attached to help Roy haul hay to the barn. Because he could not reach the floor throttle with his foot, Bob used the hand throttle and began moving the truck by letting the clutch out easily. When the process did not work smoothly, Roy was often thrown from the back of the truck. Some of Bob's friends suggest that driving the Model-A gave him a lifelong love of speed and the thrill of flying on land.[30]

Roy's ancient truck was a legend in the neighborhood. It rattled so badly that when he began the trip from Bill McCormick's farm where his cattle grazed, the family could hear him approaching. Dorothy knew her husband was coming and began putting dinner on the table. By the time Roy and the Model-A arrived, dinner was waiting.

In grade school at Cherry Valley, Bob was active in every sport the school offered.

Three

LEARNING ABOUT HARD WORK

BOB LOVED LIFE AND THE PEOPLE AROUND HIM. He knew everyone in his small school. "He was so popular," his sister, Joanne, remembered, "because he was always trying to help others."[1]

Bob's social life revolved around the Duvall Methodist Church, the largest church in town. There were only two other churches in Duvall, a Catholic parish and a Dutch Reformed Church.

Bob and his cousin, Vida Wainscott, usually played major roles in church programs. Bob sang in the church choir directed by his aunt, Alta Wainscott. Holidays were celebrated in huge fashion at the church. Picnics celebrated any worthy event, and there were parties to keep teenagers out of trouble on Halloween. For fun, it was not unusual for two dozen Methodist youngsters to camp out on the banks of the nearby river on Friday and Saturday nights and get up early enough on Sunday to be on time for Sunday School.[2]

The Duvall Methodist Church was a wood frame structure with hardwood benches as pews. The parishioners had installed striking stained-glass windows, and there was a steeple with a loud bell inside. The church was near the center of town at Main and Stella streets, just one block from the Funk home.[3]

When Bob was 11 years old, the Methodist church in Duvall became affiliated with the Evangelical Methodist Church (EMC), founded in Memphis, Tennessee, in 1946. The local Duvall Methodist congregation agreed with EMC founder, Dr. J. H. Hamblen, that mainstream Methodist church leaders in America had grown liberal and had strayed from the long-held belief that the Bible was inspired by God. To preserve the distinctive Biblical doctrines of the primitive Methodist church, the new group was formed.[4]

Hamblen was the father of Stuart Hamblen, the writer of 225 gospel songs, including some of Christendom's most famous hymns, "Until Then," "It Is No Secret," "How Big Is God?," and "Known Only to Him." Before his career as a hymn writer, Stuart Hamblen, the host of one of the West Coast's most popular afternoon radio shows, was converted during Billy Graham's first crusade in Los Angeles, California, in 1949. The story of the younger Hamblen's conversion swept the area and resulted in Graham's crusade in Los Angeles being extended.[5]

At about the same time his local church was changing affiliations, Bob, his cousins, and members of his youth group rode a rented bus from Duvall to Taft Stadium in Seattle for the Billy Graham Crusade. Bob's pastor, Oscar Renberg, heard Reverend Graham was coming to Seattle and took the opportunity to introduce the youth of the church to Graham's preaching.

The Seattle crusade, one of Graham's first city-wide crusades, was directed by Willis Graham Haymaker, the son of Presbyterian missionaries who served in Indian Territory, later Oklahoma, before the outbreak of malaria forced their return to the eastern United States.[6]

Roy and Dorothy Funk in 1954.

It was a night of decision for Bob, who answered Reverend Graham's call for salvation. Bob believed in God. His faith was strong because of his mother's teachings. He had learned Biblical principles in Sunday School from dedicated teachers. Bob was also influenced in his early life by his pastor, Francis Pitcher. Reverend Pitcher had been at the Duvall church since 1947, and after a two-year assignment in another town, returned to the church after its change of affiliation to the Evangelical Methodist Church.

Sitting on a folding chair in the middle of the football field at Taft Stadium in Seattle was an unlikely place for Bob to make a decision that he believes changed his life for the good, forever. As Reverend Graham closed his sermon and asked members of the large crusade audience to accept Christ, Bob was among the first to begin the trek toward the area in front of the platform.

A half century later, Bob remembered the moment, "I felt I had to go forward. I knew about Christ, but I had never accept-

Both Bob and his sister, Joanne, took piano lessons in Duvall. Bob quit after two years but Joanne persisted and eventually became the church pianist at the Duvall Methodist Church.

ed Him as my personal Savior. I sincerely believed that if I did not make Christ the center of my life at that time, I surely would be damning my future. I even thought that our bus might leave the road and crash on the way home that night if I had not answered the call."[7] Even though Bob's theology was that of an 11-year-old boy, he perceived that something inside was tugging at him to make the life-changing decision.

Bob was not alone in making a decision for Christ at Billy Graham's Seattle crusade. Official records kept by the evangelist show 6,785 decisions made during the crusade. More than 400,000 Seattle area residents attended the crusade.[8]

For days after his conversion experience, Bob read and reread the literature he received at the Billy Graham Crusade. He was discipled by his pastor. Reverend Pitcher was one of the best preachers Bob ever heard. Bob remembered, "He was evangelistically oriented in a soft, smooth way. He was so compassionate and loved everyone in his congregation. He was one of the smoothest preachers you could hear anywhere."[9]

Even though Bob did not realize it at the time, his emerging Christian beliefs were aligned with the tenets of the Evangelical Methodist Church (EMC). As a teenager, Bob put great stock in keeping promises. If he promised a friend he would be somewhere at a certain time, he fulfilled the promise. The church, Bob later learned, preached that promises are the voluntary bond of unity. Official EMC statements of faith said that while all believers share common bonds of their connection to Christ, a cohesive, effective local church could be possible only if a diverse group of individuals joined together in a common cause, made promises to each other, and kept the promises.[10]

One of Bob's mentors was Ed Peterson who attended the Duvall Methodist Church. For years Ed would drop his wife off at church and head for a nearby tavern. He later became active in the church because of the efforts of Bob's pastor, Francis Pitcher, who witnessed to him while fishing along the banks of the Snoqualmie River. The informal conversations paid off. One night, Peterson was so stricken with the need for salvation that he knelt at his bedside and accepted Christ. Bob remembered, "Ed was a vibrant, zealous missionary in our town. He would tell anyone what had happened to his life." Bob watched Peterson's life change and faithfulness in attending church. It inspired Bob to become a positive witness like him.[11]

Life at the Methodist church also introduced the Funk children to music. Both Joanne and Bob were "forced" to take piano lessons first from Mrs. Wright and then from Mrs. Campbell, a piano teacher from California, who lived adjacent to the church. She was a good teacher. Joanne learned so well that she became the church pianist at age 12. Bob began his piano lessons in the seventh grade, but only lasted two years. While Joanne practiced consistently, Bob did not—he wanted to be outside playing softball and basketball.[12]

At the end of the eighth grade, Bob and his parents had to decide which high school he would attend. Because of a dispute over taxation districts, students who attended high school at Monroe, 10 miles to the north, had to catch the school bus at the Snohomish County line two miles from Duvall. The other choice was to attend high school in Carnation, 10 miles to the south. Carnation was a rough logging town with a reputation for having many students who were heavy drinkers. Bob, because he believed Carnation students might treat his conservative views with disdain, chose Monroe High School, which had about 200 students and was the larger of the two schools.[13]

From his first day at Monroe, Bob became active in sports and Future Farmers of America (FFA). As a freshman, he made the high school tennis team, although he had to force his way onto the

RIGHT: When Roy Funk was not working, he enjoyed fishing for steelhead in the Snoqualmie River.

BELOW: Bob and his cousins celebrate their eighth grade graduation in 1954 at a party in the basement of the Duvall Methodist Church. Left to right, Susie Herman, Bob, Dick Trim, and Vida Wainscott.

Bob's only transportation around Duvall in his early teen years was a bicycle.

five-man squad. To make the team, Bob had to defeat upperclass-men in singles matches. He did, and the coach reluctantly made him part of the team. Bob lettered in tennis for four years—the last four-year letterman Monroe High School ever had.[14]

Bob was not a natural athlete. He did not look like an athlete. He was tall and "skinny as a bone," but he outworked other team members and lettered in two sports. He often practiced until

5:30 or 6:00 p.m. to make sure he was the best at whatever sport he was playing. He enjoyed the competition and made many friends on the high school team and on other teams in the valley. He also was close to his cousins, Jerry Wainscott and Richard "Dick" Trim, who were excellent athletes and very competitive. Bob accepted his nickname, "Skunk," which rhymed with Funk.

Even in high school, Joanne continued to mother her little brother. When Bob became involved in extracurricular activities at school and needed to stay after class, his mother was upset because the family did not have enough money to pay for gasoline for an extra 20-mile round trip. Dorothy told Joanne, "If you let him stay at school anymore, I'll use the willow switch on you!" Joanne knew how much her brother wanted to be involved in after-school events, so she said, "Okay, I'll just take the spanking." Fortunately, Dorothy never punished Joanne for leaving Bob at school.[15]

The vocational agriculture instructor and FFA sponsor at Monroe High School, Berlin Vance, made a significant impact upon young Bob's life. Bob enrolled in FFA for all four years of high school. He was on the judging team and evaluated potatoes and other crops, cattle, hogs, and sheep. He proudly wore the blue FFA jacket emblazoned with gold emblems and his name.[16]

Bob's best friends in FFA were Les Kinney and John Helm. The three spent much of their time cruising the streets of Monroe and Sultan and generally "hanging out." Kinney, still a farmer decades after graduating from high school with Bob, remembered their time in FFA, "We took farming seriously. We did pretty well on dairy, potatoes, and forage judging teams. It was a great way to learn real-life, practical farming techniques."[17]

An interest in farming and a common set of values put Bob, Les, and John together as friends for life. Bob, who was voted

ABOVE: Bob's first cow and calf that became his project for Future Farmers of America.

LEFT: An aerial view of the Hanisch farm outside Duvall, Washington, where Bob worked many years and dreamed of owning his own dairy herd.

most likely to succeed in his high school class, also was the best bowler of the threesome. "Bob was fun-loving, highly ethical, generous, hardworking, spiritual, and a true friend," Helm remembered.[18]

Bob's family did not have enough money to buy expensive livestock for FFA projects. However, Bob did use his savings from working weekends at Adolph Hanisch's dairy farm to buy a Holstein heifer when he was a freshman. Bob used the animal as his FFA project for the remainder of high school. Feeding and working with his FFA animals gave Bob a deep passion for raising livestock.

From age 14, Bob was a hard worker at the Hanisch farm. His first job was to ride on the back of a hay baler and tie strings around bales that the machine did not successfully complete. For eight to ten hours a day in the harvest season, he would ride the baler with dust blowing in his face. After the baling was done for the day, Bob helped monitor the DeLavel milking machines and cleaned manure from calf pens. After cleaning the pens, he often washed the walls of the milking barns. Frequent inspections demanded cleanliness in dairies.[19]

Before he was able to legally drive, Bob traveled back and forth to work at the farm on a Cushman scooter. About a week after he received his driver's license at age 16, he bought a 1951 black Ford sedan with large white-wall tires and white skirts. The gear shift on the steering column was interchangeable so he could flip sides and shift with his left hand during a date when he had his right arm around a girl. Bob also saved money for two years to buy his sister, Joanne, a Lane cedar chest for her high school graduation.[20]

Bob "dated around" for several years. He had known Nedra Pitcher, the daughter of his pastor, since she was five, but did not consider her a real girlfriend.[21] However, during his senior year, Bob broke the ice and asked Nedra to go with him to the church Valentine's Day banquet. "She was pretty, she always carried her shoulders back, and was very erect and proper," Bob remembered.[22] Bob and Nedra began a casual dating relationship that would ebb and flow for several years.

Nedra had learned hospitality skills from her mother, Ruth Pitcher, to host guests in the pastorate. When evangelists came to Duvall, Nedra and her sister helped prepare meals while her parents were entertaining.

Like Bob, Nedra grew up in a very conservative family. Her mother did not wear rings and did not allow her children to dance or play cards.[23]

Bob began thinking about his future during his senior year in high school. Because of a series of life experiences, he wanted to pursue three directions in his life. He wanted to be a preacher, a farmer, and a businessman.

The desire to be an Evangelical Methodist preacher grew from the time he was converted at age 11 and was shaped by his admiration of Reverend Pitcher, his pastor and mentor. Reverend Pitcher urged Bob and all members of the youth group to consider Christian service, either full time or part time. At age 15, Bob committed to Christian service, to go wherever God called him. Bob said, "I promised God that if He wanted me to go to the mission field, I would go." Once Bob made the commitment to a life of Christian service, he felt a burden had been lifted from him.[24]

Bob's positive experience in working on the Hanisch farm and in completing projects in FFA made him want to be a farmer. Additionally, his experience with the business side of farming and observing the successful dairy operation run by Adolph Hanisch gave him the idea that he might pursue a business career. Watching the operation of the grocery store

Bob graduated from high school in 1958.

where his mother worked also encouraged Bob to consider retail business. After all, he was outgoing, loved people, and enjoyed helping others.

Frankly, Bob was confident that he could do all three things at once. His boss and cousin, Adolph Hanisch, did not share his confidence. He told Bob, "You're dreaming! It's impossible to have three occupations at once."[25]

Fiercely independent, Bob graduated from Monroe High School in May, 1958, and headed to college. He was determined to pursue his dreams.

Bob began wearing hats early in life. He did not feel "dressed up" for church or college activities without wearing a hat.

Four

OFF TO COLLEGE

BOB'S MOTHER WAS DETERMINED that he attend college. She regretted not continuing her own higher education and wanted Bob to get ahead in life.

However, Bob's parents had no extra money for his college education. When he was looking for a school to attend, Bob kept that fact in mind. In his senior year of high school, he applied for scholarships and worked every possible hour at the Hansich farm to save money. During the summer before he began classes at Seattle Pacific College (SPC), now Seattle Pacific University, he worked as many as 80 hours a week milking cows, cleaning pens, and helping out where needed on the farm.[1]

Bob labored from sun up to after sun down many days and saved $800 that summer. With the savings and scholarships from the Rotary Club and Future Farmers of America, he was able to afford the $800 for tuition and room and board at SPC.

Bob chose SPC because it was close to home and because his pastor and future father-in-law, Reverend Pitcher, had attended the school. SPC was located near downtown Seattle. The college was founded as the Seattle Seminary in 1891 by the Oregon and Washington Conference of the Free Methodist Church. Methodists in the region wanted a college to train young people for missionary service. The school became Seattle Pacific College in 1915.[2]

SPC began on five acres on the north side of Seattle's Queen Anne Hill. The land was donated from the garden plot of Nils B. Peterson, a Seattle homesteader, who served as an early trustee of the seminary. The seminary opened with two faculty members and 34 students in a college preparatory curriculum. By the 1930s, there were 400 students. In the years following World War II, SPC expanded its offerings and tripled in size.[3]

Bob enrolled with a major in religion and a minor in business at a time when SPC was growing, both in the number of students and in the physical plant.[4]

Bob closely identified with the published mission statement of SPC and its president, Dr. C. Hoyt Watson. The goal of the school was to educate young men and women of competence and character. The curriculum and resources were intended to shape graduates to be effective and positive agents of change in the world. College leaders wanted their students to be "thinking Christians" who were able to speak clearly and intelligently about their convictions.[5]

The SPC campus was only 25 miles from Bob's home in Duvall, so he usually left his college dormitory life on Friday afternoons and headed home for the weekend. He enjoyed seeing how fast his black Ford Deluxe could travel on the one-mile flat stretch of highway coming into Duvall. His dormitory roommate, Ernie Trim, remembered, "Bob liked to come down the hill at breakneck speed and see how far he could coast toward town."[6]

One of Bob's "speed" and "coast" experiments ended badly one Friday afternoon. As the speedometer on the Deluxe began to rise, the universal joint broke and the drive shaft literally dropped onto the highway. Bob and Trim had to walk the rest of the way to Duvall.[7]

Bob continued to work as much as possible at the Hanisch farm, had regular dates with Nedra, and attended Duvall Evangelical Methodist Church on Sunday mornings. Bob liked the familiarity of his hometown on weekends. The newness of the large city of Seattle and the size of SPC made him a bit uncomfortable and slow to make friends in his first semester. Even though SPC was a small school by college standards, it was certainly much larger than his high school graduating class of 56 students.[8]

Bob had difficulty with some of his early basic courses. One of his first hurdles was a philosophy class taught by a high-browed professor. Bob was accustomed to practical education but the professor wanted to ask questions such as, "If a tree falls in the forest, and no one hears it, does it make any noise?" Bob's answer was, "Who cares? It doesn't matter if it makes noise or not."

When Bob registered a score of 25 on the first test in the philosophy class, he knew he was in deep trouble. What he did not know was that the students were being graded on the curve. Bob was accustomed to his high school grading system of fixed percentages. He thought 25 surely was a failing grade, so he chose not to study for the final exam.[9]

That was a mistake. He made 37 on the final exam and received a D in the course. His professor told him he had a C-plus going into the final exam, but his poor performance on the final dropped his overall grade. Bob's grade point for the first semester was 1.72, slightly below the college requirement of maintaining a 1.75 grade point to remain eligible for admission.

After the first quarter—SPC operated on a three-quarter annual basis—Bob was placed on probation. By working hard and having a better attitude about studying, he soon raised his grade point average. He gave up time with friends for extra study. When he was confused about a particular issue, he stayed after class and asked his professors for clarification.[10]

With his summer savings, Bob had sufficient money to remain a student at SPC without student loans. He was making $2 an hour on the Hanisch farm and his mother would occasionally slip him a $20 bill to help with gas money and meals.

Bob continued his participation in sports at SPC. At first, Bob's above average tennis skills were not appreciated by other tennis players at the college. "I was a tennis kid from a small town, coming into the big city with all the city-slickers and rich kids who played tennis at some of the big high schools," he remembered.[11] The veterans of the SPC tennis program thought Bob was encroaching on their territory.

To make the team, Bob had to tackle what was called the "ladder" system. He was required to challenge the next person in rank above him and move up the ladder. After a few practice sessions, he challenged the number five player and beat him. The tennis coach was not extremely happy about Bob's success because he had handpicked the team. The day before the season's first match, Bob again challenged the number five player. Bob won again and was reluctantly given a spot on the team. By the time Bob was a junior, he had risen to the number one spot on the SPC tennis team.[12]

Nedra graduated from high school in 1960, moved to Seattle into an apartment, and took a clerical job with a pharmaceutical company. She had no money for college and frankly did not want to be a school teacher or nurse. At that time, many young women saw no need for a college education unless they wanted to enter one of those two professions.[13]

Bob and Nedra's dating relationship remained in limbo. There was no serious talk of marriage and Bob occasionally went on dates with other girls. In his final two years of college, he became heavily involved in campus organizations and college activities.

He toured with the college choir in concerts all over the West Coast and was president of the choir his final year of college.

One event placed a severe strain on Bob and Nedra's relationship. In Bob's senior year, the SPC homecoming queen asked him to be her escort. Bob knew her from choir and accepted the invitation. The problem arose because Bob did not tell Nedra. When Nedra saw their photograph on the front page of the Seattle newspaper, she was "a bit upset."[14]

Bob was positively influenced by many of his professors at SPC. One professor who made a significant impact on Bob's religious training was Joe Davis. Davis was, in Bob's words, a "down-to-earth good person." Davis was a realist and consistently gave his students practical tips on the ministry, not just the religious theory needed for a career in the ministry. He hosted a student Bible study in his home on Wednesday evenings and related well to his students.[15]

Bob liked Davis personally and agreed with his real-world outlook on preaching. Bob said, "He was very practical, and I needed that. I came from a small town and was a very practical person and not that much of a deep, intellectual student."[16] Davis' practical approach came from his experience as a Methodist minister and missionary.

As Bob approached the end of his bachelor's degree study, he still carried the dream of being an Evangelical Methodist preacher, a businessman, and a farmer. He had limited experience in the pulpit; although he occasionally filled in at his home church when Reverend Pitcher was away.

As Bob began to appear before church groups, he began doubting his ability to stand before congregations to preach. He remembers his first sermons as "not very good." He was a procrastinator and admittedly did not spend enough time in preparation for the sermons. His professors at SPC told him that 10-15 hours of study were required to adequately prepare for each sermon. Because of his activities and work, Bob seldom had more than a couple of hours to study and prepare.[17]

Even though Bob questioned his skills as a preacher, he was committed to his relationship with Christ and moved ahead with plans to attend seminary. He consulted his advisors and professors at SPC. A popular Methodist seminary which many of the SPC professors attended was Asbury Theological Seminary in Kentucky. It was common for SPC graduates to continue their studies at Asbury. However, when Bob was informed that attending Asbury would cost nearly $1,200 a year, he looked elsewhere.[18]

In the spring of 1962, a few months before graduation, Bob talked to a former SPC student who was attending New College Seminary, part of the prestigious University of Edinburgh in Scotland. Bob learned that Edinburgh was not only one of the romantic cities of Europe, but that the seminary faculty included some of the greatest theologians in the world, including Dr. James Stewart. Bob was familiar with many of Stewart's books such as *In His Name*.[19]

Despite the caliber of education, the deciding factor for Bob was not the prestige of the seminary in Scotland—it was a financial decision. Bob discovered that he could attend school at the University of Edinburgh, including traveling back and forth to Europe, for less money than he would be required to pay at Asbury in Kentucky.

Bob discussed the idea with his parents. His mother did not want him to be so far from home because he had never even traveled outside the United States. Bob's father thought attending seminary in Europe was foolish. But when Bob told his parents about the cheap tuition of $220 a year and the inexpensive living arrangements and airfare, they reluctantly gave their blessing.

Another consideration was Bob's relationship with Nedra. Even though they had dated for five years, there was no long-term commitment, at least from Bob's perspective. Nedra knew that Bob was going to seminary somewhere, so it did not matter whether he was in Kentucky or Scotland. Both places were a long way from King County, Washington.[20]

LEFT: Bob at a family outing in Duvall during his college years. *Courtesy Dick Trim.*

Bob graduated from Seattle Pacific College in Seattle, Washington, in May, 1962. Left to right, Roy Funk, Dorothy Funk, Bob, and his cousin Adolph Hanisch.

Attending seminary at the University of Edinburgh was a great opportunity for Bob with seeing Europe as an added benefit. This builing is one of the Pollack Halls of Residence at the University of Edinburgh. *Courtesy Erin Moore.*

Five

EDINBURGH

BOB'S DECISION TO ATTEND SEMINARY at the University of Edinburgh gave him the opportunity of a lifetime. He was able to attend one of the world's finest seminaries and travel in Europe. However, just getting to Scotland was an adventure for the novice traveler.[1]

Before Bob traveled to Scotland he spent the summer working on the Hannisch farm and saved nearly $900, sufficient money to pay his seminary tuition, airfare, and room and board for the entire first year of seminary.

Nedra and Bob's parents saw him off at the Seattle airport on September 19, 1962. On the last leg of the American Airlines flight to London, England, Bob sat beside a young English man whose brother was a pastor in the British capital. Since Bob did not have a place to stay in London before he took another flight the following day, Bob's new friend offered his brother's parsonage. He promised to call his brother once they arrived in London.[2]

When arrangements were made, Bob took the London Tube and followed specific instructions to get off at a certain subway station. Carrying two heavy suitcases, Bob climbed from the underground station and found himself in a tough inner-city

East End London neighborhood. He hailed a taxi that took him to the parsonage where he was to spend the night.

Frightened by his surroundings, Bob pounded on the front door of the parsonage, but there was no answer. He knocked for several minutes to no avail. His taxi was gone and his only option was to walk to any business that remained open to call the minister who lived in the parsonage. For safety, Bob walked in the middle of the street, rather than on the dark sidewalk. It was 11:00 p.m. and several drunks were being kicked out of pubs that closed at that hour.

Bob found a pay phone and called the Methodist parsonage. He could hear the minister answer, but the minister could not hear Bob who did not know that in the British Isles, money had to be deposited in a pay phone after the person on the other end of the line answered. Bob obviously looked helpless to one of the pub patrons who, even though in an intoxicated state, recognized this young American boy needed help. The stranger dialed the parsonage, inserted the coin in the proper manner, and Bob grabbed the phone, yelling, "Please don't hang up, whatever you do."[3]

The minister explained that he lived in such a crime-ridden neighborhood and had been robbed so many times, he never answered knocks on the door at night. Bob walked back to the parsonage and this time was allowed to enter to spend the night.

The next morning, Bob took the Tube back to the airport and flew to Manchester, England, to visit with Dr. Don Demeray, one of his former professors at Seattle Pacific College, who was completing his doctorate studies at the University of Manchester. It was comforting to Bob that someone who knew him from Washington was in that part of the world.[4]

After a few hours in Manchester, Bob flew in a small British Airways passenger plane to Edinburgh. He arrived at the seminary admissions office a few minutes before closing time at 5:00 p.m. and asked for information about renting a room for the night. He was told to take a city bus to another section of Edinburgh about five miles from the university where a family rented housing, called "digs," to students.[5]

The next morning, Bob walked around the University of Edinburgh campus. He was overwhelmed at the magnificence of the old buildings, the beauty of the carefully landscaped grounds, and the storied history of the institution.

The University of Edinburgh was established by a Royal Charter granted by King James VI in 1582. It was the fourth university in Scotland in a period when the much more populous and richer England had only two colleges. By the 18th century, Edinburgh was one of Europe's principal universities and a leading center of the European Enlightenment.[6]

The university existed in a hodgepodge of buildings until the early nineteenth century when permanent, architecturally beautiful structures housed classes and offices. While walking through the maze of historic buildings, Bob found the seminary which was located in a building known as New College, originally built as a Free Church college in the 1840s. The building had been the home of the School of Divinity since 1935.[7]

Within the next few days, classes began and Bob became familiar with the other famous buildings on the campus. Teviot Row House was the oldest student union building in the world. The handsomely-restored MyIne's Court student residence stood at the head of Edinburgh's Royal Mile. The university library was Scotland's largest and oldest library.[8]

Bob continued to learn about the school during the first few weeks. In a student orientation session, Bob was told that the university's fundamental mission was simply the advancement and dissemination of knowledge and understanding. He learned about some of the university's famous graduates, including Sir Walter Scott; Robert Louis Stevenson, who founded the student newspaper, *Student*; and Sir Arthur Conan Doyle, creator of Sherlock Holmes.[9]

The School of Divinity was unlike any academic setting with which Bob was familiar. He had attended elementary and high school in tiny school districts, graduated from a relatively small college, and was now thrust into classes in one of the world's most prestigious venues for religious training.[10] The School of Divinity had long been one of the world's centers of reformed theology and was home to distinguished theologians and Biblical scholars such as H.R. Mackintosh, John Baillie, T.F. Torrance, James Barr, and James Stewart.[11]

As soon as Bob settled into his class work, he began venturing out into the city of Edinburgh. What he found was an ancient city known for its architecture, a city rich with social, cultural, learning, and sporting events. The Edinburgh Castle dominated the city's skyline from atop a hill. The splendor of the city's heritage was everywhere. At that time, nearly 300,000 people lived in Edinburgh which, because of its architecture, was often called the "Athens of the North." The city was home to one of the world's largest arts festival that drew more than one million people each year. Edinburgh also was home to the Scottish Parliament and was a gateway to the coastline, hills, and open country of the Scottish Highlands.[12]

For $30 a week, Bob rented a room and was provided breakfast and evening meals. He lived in his first "digs" for six weeks and met other students who became lifelong friends. Hugh Mackie was an engineering student who was interested in visiting nearby pubs while Bob was looking for a church to attend. They made a deal—Bob would go with Mackie to the pubs and Mackie would go with Bob to church. Even though Bob did not condone the use of alcohol, he did not mind going to the pubs because that was where the best food was served. Scots generally dined in pubs, not in restaurants.[13]

After six weeks, Bob found another living arrangement with a red-headed Canadian couple, the Fraziers, who were renting an apartment from a missionary who was on assignment in India. The couple had a spare room and asked Bob to occupy it. Hugh Frazier was a student in the School of Divinity and owned an automobile, a great advantage for Bob whose sole source of transportation for his first few weeks in Scotland was the excellent city bus system. Mrs. Frazier did not work outside the home and spent her time caring for their one-year-old son.[14]

Bob's new home was in the south section of Edinburgh, about five miles from the seminary. His room was in an old block apartment complex that had no central air conditioning or heat. Heat was provided by a "shilling meter," a wall heater that could be turned on only by depositing a British coin, the shilling. On cold Scottish winter nights, the heater was not powerful enough to raise the temperature beyond 62 degrees Fahrenheit. A shilling, at the time worth about 20 cents, had to be deposited every 30 minutes.[15]

After Bob had been at the University of Edinburgh two months, he joined the school's basketball team which was made up of mostly American students. Bob had not played competitive basketball at Seattle Pacific College but decided he could make the Edinburgh team without much difficulty. He was tall, with long arms, and could go "over the top" on smaller defenders.

Basketball was a minor sport in Europe where soccer and football ruled. Because very few people attended college basketball games, the contests were played in dimly-lit, small gymnasiums. Although fans were rare, one Scottish girl, Moyra, became interested in Bob. She religiously followed the team, and they began dating. Bob occasionally heard from Nedra, but the long-distance relationship had grown cold.[16]

The basketball team traveled the British Isles taking on other college, university, and military teams. The team did well, losing only to the University of London and to a United States Air Force team in Edinburgh. In the loss to the University of London, Bob played against a young man with an eight-foot wingspan. Bob said, "I couldn't get around him." Although it was a tough night, Bob scored 15 points.

The highlight of the basketball season for Bob was beating the team from Oxford University. Bob labeled the contest "a game between the little upstart kids from Edinburgh and the big Rhodes Scholar kids out of Oxford."[17]

Bob's "wicked" hook shot, that he could hit either right-handed or left-handed, won him most valuable player honors on the Edinburgh basketball team. The honor, called "The Blue," meant he was entitled to wear a special blazer and necktie that told other students he was the most valuable player of some sport played at the university.

At the end of the first of three annual class sessions in the School of Divinity, Bob was invited by the Fraziers to take a driving trip through Europe to the Holy Land. Bob had saved a small amount of money and was able to join the trip for $135. Bob, the Fraziers, and another couple began their 10-day journey in a Ford Falcon station wagon. They took a ferry to the European continent and drove through Germany, Switzerland, and Austria. They went behind the Iron Curtain into Yugoslavia and Bulgaria that had been open to foreign traffic for only a few months.[18]

Once the travelers left the relatively good roads of modern Western Europe, they found horrible driving conditions in the countries they visited in Eastern Europe. In Bulgaria and Yugoslavia, they encountered chug holes sometimes two to three feet deep. They could drive only in daytime hours and someone had to be on constant lookout for dangers in the roadway.

Bob and the others stopped in Zegreb, Yugoslavia, to deliver cigarettes to the brother of one of his neighbors in Edinburgh. They arrived in Zegreb, a city of more than one million people, after dark. Bob was astounded at the primitive conditions of Eastern Europe. From a hillside, he could see only a dozen or so lights in an area where hundreds of thousands of people lived and worked. They found the home where they were promised the night's lodging and parked the Ford Falcon under a street-light to protect it from thieves.[19]

Yugoslavia was suffering under the dictatorship of Marshall Tito. Bob saw how the people were adversely affected by communism. Even though his host had a good job, there was only a bed, a couch, a dresser, and a kitchen table in the entire house. Under communism, everyone was equally poor.[20]

The following morning, they headed south toward the Holy Land. Outside Dubrovnek, the second-largest city in Yugoslavia, Bob saw women washing their family's clothing in a river in freezing temperatures. He thought to himself, "Thank God, I was born in America!"[21]

In Dubrovnek, the travelers found a hotel where they were greeted by a cashier protected by a wire cage. The lady wanted their passports to assure she would be paid and her guests would not escape during the night. Bob was concerned about leaving his American passport in a communist country, but he had no choice. There was only one light bulb on the entire third story of the hotel.

In the pitch darkness of the night, there was a knock at the door. Hugh Frazier opened the door but could see no one. At 2:00 a.m., there was another knock at the door. Again, no one was there. Bob and Frazier used the sparse furniture in the hotel room to barricade the door. They were sure they were being harassed because they were Canadian and American citizens. None of the travelers slept very much that night.[22]

The next day the journey continued into Turkey where a new danger lay ahead. Large trucks ruled the Turkish highways. The trucks sometimes played "chicken" with each other. Overturned trucks in the ditches alongside the highways were sad reminders of these deadly games. They found a better hotel in Ankara, the capital of Turkey. For dinner, they had skewered beef, although, Bob remembered, "It was tougher than shoe leather."[23]

Bob especially enjoyed visiting the ancient Turkish city of Tarsus where he saw the amphitheater in which the Apostle Paul preached. However, poverty also was rampant in Turkey. By the time Bob and his friends returned to their car, it was surrounded by more than 100 children begging for money.

The ten-day journey ended on Christmas Eve in Bethlehem. It was a special spiritual experience for Bob to observe Christmas at the Church of the Nativity in the village where Jesus Christ was born. The group stayed in a YMCA and toured the sights around Jerusalem including the area where Christ is believed to have been crucified.[24]

On Christmas Eve, Bob talked by telephone to his mother who gave him some shocking news—Nedra had gotten engaged. Bob learned that the young man had begun attending the Duvall Evangelical Methodist Church a few weeks after Bob left for Scotland. The two began dating, but no one, including Bob's mother, had told him.[25]

Even though Bob and Nedra had never talked about marriage, his feelings were hurt. He did not blame Nedra for going on with her life. He understood that there had been no commitment between them before he left for seminary. However, Bob was upset because Nedra had not told him of the engagement herself.

While attending seminary in Scotland, Bob grew long sideburns and a goatee.

Bob sat down and wrote Nedra a letter explaining that he understood his failure in expressing any commitment to her. He also wished a happy life for Nedra. For some reason, Bob did not mail the letter. Instead, he hid it in a safe place so he could deliver it and talk to Nedra one-on-one when he went home.

Even though the disturbing news about Nedra came while Bob was in Jerusalem, he decided to make the most of his visit to the Holy Land. He remembered, "to walk where Christ walked in the Garden of Gethsemane and to see the wall around the old temple made the Bible come alive. The stories blossomed in front of me."

A special moment was when Bob was baptized by his landlord, Hugh Frazier, in the Jordan River, in the same river and place where Christ was baptized by John the Baptist. Frazier was ordained as a pastor of a church in Canada before he came to study at the University of Edinburgh.[26]

After a week in the Holy Land, Bob and the others began the driving trip back to Scotland. He settled back into class work and completed the basketball season. Reeling from the news that Nedra was planning to be married soon, he thought about asking Moyra to marry him. He put that idea away for the moment, but began to seriously consider his future.[27]

Bob purchased a light green Volkswagen GB in Great Britain and, thinking he may not again have such an opportunity in his lifetime, decided to tour Europe with three friends from seminary.

A COLD SCOTTISH WINTER

IN THE COLD OF THE SCOTTISH WINTER in Edinburgh, Bob contemplated his future as a Methodist preacher. He was not overly confident in his ability to stand before a congregation and speak. Every time he tried to preach, he was plagued with concerns that he was not adequately prepared and was extremely uncomfortable delivering the sermon.[1]

The cold weather was getting to Bob. It was much colder than the damp coldness he experienced growing up in the state of Washington. Even though Bob had worked outside on the farm during the Washington winters, the Scottish winter was almost unbearable. He wore long underwear to bed and was still "frozen in the morning." There were not enough covers for the bed and on many mornings, ice covered the windows. During Bob's only winter in Edinburgh, the city experienced 33 consecutive days of freezing temperatures.

Bob tried to study at a tiny desk in his room, but the bitter cold made it nearly impossible to concentrate for very long. Instead, he went to one of two places in the city that he knew would be warm. One place he frequented was the National Library which maintained the temperature in its study halls at about 70 degrees. "With an overcoat," Bob recalled, "I could stay warm and study well."[2]

The other warm spot was in the ping pong room near the chapel. To get warm, Bob and fellow students often skipped chapel and played ping pong. The activity broke the cold that gripped the students who were sometimes chastised for missing chapel services. The classrooms in the School of Divinity were not heated. Bob and others listened to lectures and tried to take notes with cumbersome, but warm, gloves on their hands.

The Scottish people were accustomed to the cold. They were a hearty people and were prepared for the frigid weather with their wool scarves and coats. But the cold went right through Bob. He weighed only 142 pounds and had no "insulation" to protect him from the cold weather.[3]

During the cold nights and depressingly short days of the winter, Bob wondered what he should do about his future. At the end of the second trimester in March he seriously considered quitting school. He again doubted his abilities as a preacher.

There was a four-week vacation before the third trimester began. After that short term, finals were given that would decide the entire year's grade in each class. Bob had focused on basketball and thought he surely had not studied enough to pass many of his courses. The English system did not compensate for a mediocre effort—a student either passed or failed each class.

Bob thought that if he chose to return to the United States and work on his master's degree at Seattle Pacific College, he should first travel in Europe. He had no idea whether or not he would again have such an opportunity in his lifetime. He asked his mother to borrow $1,280 from a bank in Duvall for the purchase of a new Volkswagen Beetle in London. Dorothy agreed and sent the money. Soon Bob was the proud owner of a light green Volkswagen sporting a GB emblem, unique to Volkswagens sold in Great Britain.[4]

With his own transportation, Bob made a huge decision—he would skip the final trimester and take an extended driving trip through Europe with three friends from seminary.

On the night before Bob left, he almost asked Moyra to marry him, but did not. Instead, she informed him that she was immigrating to the United States shortly and would be visiting a relative in San Francisco, California. They agreed to meet in San Francisco in the early summer and talk about their future.[5]

The first stop on Bob's European tour was London. It was a typical foggy night when Bob and his friends drove to a hotel. The next day, they drove to Folkstone, England, and took the ferry across the English Channel to France.

With limited funds, Bob and the others became creative. In France, they met up with Bob's cousin, Dick Trim, who was serving in the United States Army. Trim supplied them with a trunk load of breakfast foods he took from a military commissary. For meals, they bought milk and a few potatoes from farmers or in urban markets. Potato soup and cereal were the fare for all three daily meals.[6]

They drove into southern Germany and on to Spain and Portugal, saving money by purchasing fuel at military installations. The four friends wanted to go to Gibraltar, but were running out of money. By the end of week three, Bob had only $11 to go to Gibraltar.

On one occasion, Bob narrowly missed being arrested. The friends saved on hotel expenses by sleeping outside in sleeping bags purchased in a second hand store in Edinburgh. One night, they were sleeping on a beach in Spain when Bob and the others were awakened by a bayonet pointed at their faces. The Spanish police wanted to know how many people were in Bob's party. At the time, Spanish dictator, Francisco Franco, was frightened of invasion by sea and his police forces scanned beaches for invaders.

Bob, getting out of his Volkswagen, and his cousin, Dick Trim, right, during their European trip in 1963. *Courtesy Dick Trim.*

Dick Trim remembered, "It was a tense moment as the Spanish police officers dumped our milk while laughing at us. We could not understand what they were saying but could tell from the tone of their voices that we had violated some law or rule."[7] Bob and his friends did not know it was unlawful to be on Spanish beaches at night. Following some heavy explaining, the police officer allowed them to leave.[8]

After camping on a river outside Nice, France, for a few days, Trim's leave expired, and he took a train to return to his Army unit. From the Riviera, Bob and the remaining travelers drove to Rome, Italy, and took a ferry to Greece. They visited Athens and drove through Yugoslavia, Austria, and Switzerland. Impossible as it might seem, Bob made the 1963 European trip on 25 cents a day.

In Berlin, Bob saw another graphic example of the difference in living standards in countries where capitalism flourished and nations were strangled by communism. In East Berlin everything was gray, dark, and dreary. People did not smile. However, in West Berlin, people were happy and the economy was much stronger. When Bob drove through Checkpoint Charlie to return to West Berlin, East German border guards took six hours to search his Volkswagen. Bob believed the incident was nothing but harassment of an American youth.[9]

Bob drove to Hamburg, Germany, where he had made arrangements to have his car shipped to New York City. Waiting at the American Express office in Hamburg was a letter from his mother that contained a $20 bill. Bob had told his mother the various cities he would be visiting. Once he arrived in a major city, he checked the local American Express office to see if he received any mail from home.

Bob and his friends used the $20 he received from his mother to finance another seven-day excursion into Denmark, Sweden, and Norway. He returned to Hamburg and sailed aboard the student ship to New York City. By the time he arrived in America, Bob had only $1.40 remaining.

Bob's ship arrived in New York City in the middle of June, 1963. His mother traveled cross country to meet him there, intending to drive back with him in his new car. Bob and Dorothy rented a room at the Times Square Hotel. From the hotel he could see ships coming into port. He thought surely the ship carrying his car would have arrived before him. However, he was informed that the ship was still being held in the port for customs clearance. For six days the answer from the shipping company was the same.[10]

A week's living in New York City depleted Dorothy's funds. All she had left was a Chevron gasoline credit card, but it was useless for paying hotel and food bills. On the seventh day, Bob looked out into the harbor and saw that the ship carrying his car had docked. He went to the dock and discovered his Volkswagen was only six cars from the front ramp of the dock. When he asked for his car, a union boss said it would be the next day before his men could unload the ship. Bob was upset. He and his mother were broke and wanted to leave New York City quickly.

Also upsetting Bob was the fact that the workers were busy doing something else—they were playing poker in the back room of the shipping depot. Bob pleaded with the union boss who retorted, "We're unionized here. If they don't want to get you your car, they don't have to." When Bob threatened that he and his mother would sleep on the office floor until they had his car, the workers reluctantly drove the Volkswagen off the dock. The incident gave Bob a bad taste for unions and for New York City. He did not return to the city for 38 years.[11]

Bob and Dorothy stopped at a nearby service station and used the credit card to buy a tank of gas and left New York City. They slept alongside the road in Virginia and drove the next day to Indiana to visit relatives. They borrowed $40 from relatives, the Bob Pease family, to buy food for the remainder of their trip to Duvall, Washington.

During the five-day drive from New York City to Washington, Bob talked a lot about his experiences in Scotland and the rest of Europe and about his plans to continue his education at Seattle Pacific College. Before he left Edinburgh, he had talked with an assistant registrar who basically allowed Bob to make up his own interim grades in courses that could transfer to SPC.

Bob and Dorothy also talked about Nedra. Dorothy had heard that a wedding date for Nedra and her fiancé was set for September. Bob was determined to see Nedra as soon as he could when he arrived home.[12]

Bob and Nedra were married on November 16, 1963, at the Duvall Methodist Church.

Seven

A CHANGE IN DIRECTION

NEDRA PITCHER HAD KNOWN BOB SINCE SHE WAS FIVE. They had grown close during years of high school and college dating, but the relationship waned when Bob left for seminary in Scotland without making any commitment concerning their future.[1]

After graduating from Cherry Valley Grade School, Nedra chose to attend high school at Carnation. It was primarily a financial decision. She never had an automobile throughout high school, and it was easy to catch the Tolt High School bus in front of her home.[2]

Like Bob, Nedra's life also was driven by the activities of the church which her father pastored. She was active in weekly Sunday School and youth group meetings. She attended summer camps at Rockaway Camp on the Oregon coast. She never could talk Bob into attending summer camp because the camp was normally during hay harvest season, and the camp was too structured for Bob. She said, "Camp had curfews, and Bob did not like that kind of structure."[3]

Six months before Bob received his bachelor's degree in 1962, Nedra went to work for Washington Natural Gas Company in Seattle. In the accounts department at the gas company, Nedra worked her way up from deposit clerk to head cashier. She lived in several apartments in Seattle when she was not staying with her parents and commuting to work, an hour each way. After starting her first job she bought a 1954 Plymouth for $350. It was not flashy, but the car provided a dependable way to get to and from work.[4]

When Bob returned from Scotland, Nedra's wedding to another young man was fully planned—even the wedding invitations were printed. Bob sought counsel from his sister, Joanne. He asked, "What do I do, Sis?" Joanne replied, "Go see her! She's not married yet!"[5]

Bob took his sister's advice and went to Nedra's house. They talked and Bob asked her if she was sure about marrying the other young man. Bob realized he had never made a commitment but that Nedra was his one true love. As Bob left the house, Nedra kissed him.[6]

Bob's re-entry into Nedra's life turned her world upside down. Nedra prayed for God's guidance and talked to Bob's Aunt Elnora and friends. The next night, Nedra broke off the engagement. Within a matter of days, Nedra and Bob began seeing each other again. It was as if no time had passed while Bob was in Europe. However, Bob's attitude was different—he knew he was in love with Nedra and did not want to lose her again. He immediately began talking about marriage and spending his life with her.[7]

Bob believed he should first ask Nedra's father, Reverend Pitcher, for permission to marry her. Bob and Nedra were both legally adults—he was 23, she was 21—but Bob greatly respected Reverend Pitcher and wanted his approval. When Reverend Pitcher asked, "Are you sure this is what you want to do?" Bob answered, "Yes," and his future father-in-law gave the wedding his blessing.[8]

Bob's parents, Roy and Dorothy Funk, later in life. Dorothy died on September 5, 1974. Roy died twenty years later on October 22, 1994.

Bob also had some decisions to make regarding his education. There was still a strong desire to emphasize Christian service in his life. His plans to become a preacher had been altered, but he wanted to help people. He thought that he might teach religion in a college or seminary. With his future still uncertain, he decided to pursue his master's degree at Seattle Pacific College but he first had to save money to pay for the schooling and his anticipated wedding to Nedra.[9]

Bob milked cows and worked on the Adolph Hanisch farm from before daylight until after dark. He saw Nedra almost every night after she returned from work.

Nedra and Bob were married on November 16, 1963. What they did not know at the time was that this was also the date of Statehood Day in Oklahoma, their future home. Oklahoma became the 46th state of the United States on November 16, 1907.

Reverend Pitcher officiated the wedding ceremony at the Duvall Evangelical Methodist Church. Nedra's sister, Kay, was the matron of honor. Bob's best man was Bob Friesen, a friend from Seattle Pacific College. After a reception in the fellowship hall, Bob and Nedra went on a driving trip for their honeymoon. They headed east toward Iowa to attend the wedding of

Bob's cousin, Dick Trim, who he had met up with in Europe. On the 10-day trip, they also visited another of Bob's cousins, Bob Pease, and his wife Joanna and their family.

After the honeymoon, Bob and Nedra moved into a small house on Third Street in Duvall that they had purchased from Bob's grandmother, Pearl Funk. Mrs. Funk allowed the newlyweds to pay the $3,500 purchase price in $80 monthly payments. Bob still worked on the farm, but the primary family income came from Nedra's $450 per month salary from Washington Natural Gas Company.[10]

In the summer of 1964, Bob got serious about returning to college and enrolled in the master's degree program in religion at Seattle Pacific College. In addition to wanting to continue his education and receive his master's degree, there was another consideration—his possible draft into the military. Tensions were high between the United States and the Soviet Union. There was talk of a draft of young men to fill the armed forces in case of all-out war with the Soviet Union.

Because Nedra already was working at the gas company office in Seattle, the couple decided to sell their house and find lodging closer to her work and the college campus. They found a 20-unit motel which Bob could manage in exchange for a free room. Bob attended classes until mid-afternoon then manned the front desk to check guests in. Nedra worked at the gas company all day but still found time to clean rooms and make beds.[11]

Dr. Talmadge Wilson was Bob's adviser at SPC. Wilson, a longtime missionary to the Sudan, was home on sabbatical while Bob attended the college for his master's work. Wilson, who had completely memorized seven books of the Bible, gave Bob practical advice on Christian service, emphasizing the fact that he could do much to further the cause of Christ without being a full-time preacher. This advice stuck with Bob.[12]

During his second stint at SPC, Bob made good grades. He thought he might have a chance to teach at the college, even though he would have only a master's degree. His reason was that his hero during undergraduate days, Professor Joe Davis, had only a master's degree and became a respected teacher at SPC. Bob graduated with his master's degree in religion, with a minor in business, in May, 1964, and began looking for work.

He and Nedra left the motel management position and bought an old two-story house in Duvall across the street from Bob's parents and three blocks down the street from Nedra's parents. Reverend Pitcher had retired as pastor of the church in Duvall, but was district superintendent and chairman of the foreign and Mexican missions board of the Evangelical Methodist Church.[13]

Bob thought he might want to return to farming. His cousin Adolph was getting older so Bob thought he might be able to buy the Hanisch farm. Adolph had never married and had no heirs to succeed him in ownership of the farm.[14]

Bob had worked for Adolph for 11 years and considered himself the closest family member to him. It was a mutual feeling. For years, Bob had worked holidays—Christmas, Thanksgiving, and the Fourth of July—so that Adolph could have time off from the daily grind of running the dairy. For Bob, it was natural that he follow in the farming footsteps of his cousin.

Before Bob approached Adolph about buying the farm, he visited with officials of the Federal Land Bank office in Seattle and preliminarily arranged for financing for both the land and Adolph's cattle. Bob went to Adolph and asked to buy the farm. Adolph liked the idea of his cousin taking over the farm which his parents had homesteaded, but told Bob he was not yet ready to give up total control of the operation. Although Adolph gave him a glimmer of hope by suggesting that he might sell in a couple of years, Bob was disappointed.[15]

The glimmer of hope grew faint when Bob heard the terms of Adolph's proposal. He promised that if Bob continued to work for him, he would buy replacement cows in Bob's name until the herd was renewed. Bob knew it would take six or seven years for that to happen, not fast enough in his estimation to make a better farm and improve milk production.[16]

Bob never got the Hanisch farm. After Adolph died, the property was sold and the estate divided among 21 cousins. However, while Adolph remained alive, Bob still thought he had a chance of ending up with the farm.

His idea was that he would take a job, any job, for two years in Seattle and then buy the Hanisch farm. To make that happen, he applied for jobs in Seattle at the state employment office and at a private employment agency, Acme Personnel. Bob casually knew the manager of the office, Gordon Blair, who had given his Christian testimony during one of Bob's classes at SPC.

Bob had another unusual connection with Blair. While Bob's mother, Dorothy, was a student at the University of Puget Sound, she was Blair's nanny. That fact was discovered when Blair and his wife, Jeanne, were reacquainted with Dorothy while coming to get meat from Bob at the grocery store where she worked. Blair had a unique scar on his neck from a childhood injury. When Dorothy saw the scar on Blair's neck, she instantly remembered him.[17]

When Bob went to the Acme office at Third Street and Union Avenue in downtown Seattle, he was seen by one of Blair's associates. Bob announced he was looking for any kind of work. He was sent on two interviews. The first opportunity was at a retail credit company that had a management training program. That interview was not successful.

The second interview was with Dun & Bradstreet, a global provider of company credit reports and profiles. The company offered Bob a job for $425 a month. Bob accepted the position immediately and returned to Acme to make arrangements to pay the job finder's fee. At that time, an employee who was matched by an employment service to a job paid the fee. Bob was allowed three months to pay the $200 fee.[18]

At Dun & Bradstreet, Bob was sent into the field to gather financial information from companies so his firm could develop a profile and credit report. Bob was uncomfortable being aggressive in requesting sensitive financial data from hesitant company owners. Also, he knew he was not a good writer and felt inadequate in preparing written financial profiles on companies he visited.[19]

After two months at Dun & Bradstreet, Bob expressed his feelings to Gordon Blair who promised to look for a position for Bob at Acme Personnel. Bob was so frustrated with his job, he told Blair, "I don't care what the salary is, just give me the job and I will make my way." After four interviews, Blair showed confidence in Bob's abilities and made a job for him as the fifth person in the Acme office. The salary was $375 a month. Bob knew absolutely nothing about the employment staffing business, but he was willing to learn. That attitude paved the way for Bob to make history in the business.

Eight

INSIDE WORK

WORKING LONG HOURS IN AN OFFICE SETTING was strange for Bob. For years he had labored outdoors on the farm. He was accustomed to fresh air, although one could question the quality of the air in a dairy barn where he spent hours each morning and afternoon for much of his working life.

During his first few weeks trapped in an office all day, Bob had to occasionally leave his office at Acme Personnel and walk up and down Third Avenue taking in the fresh air of Seattle. On some days, he did not know how he could handle being "cooped up" all day. Every week, however, he became more accustomed to working indoors. "If it had not been in a business helping people," Bob said, "I could not have lasted, tied to a chair for eight hours."

With a change in direction in his life away from preaching, Bob's lifelong desire to help people was being fulfilled by helping people find jobs. He was not standing before a congregation as a minister, but he was able to help individuals in need. The one-on-one contact with people looking for work gave him a special feeling. For the first time in years, his future was becoming clear to him.[1]

The new job worked out well for Bob and Nedra's transportation. Their only vehicle was the Volkswagen Bob had purchased in England. They rode together on the 55-minute journey from Duvall to downtown Seattle. Nedra let Bob off at the Acme office at Third and Union and went on to her job at the gas company six blocks away. At quitting time, she retraced her steps, picked him up, and they drove home to Duvall.[2]

Bob took his assignment at Acme Personnel seriously. He looked up to Gordon Blair and watched his every move in his operation of the employment service. Bob became aware that the industry as a whole had an image problem. Even though Acme was honest in its dealings with both potential workers and employers, many employment agencies were looking for quick profits. They lied to employers about applicants' test results and lied to applicants about the potential for a particular job.[3]

Another reason the personnel business was looked on negatively by the press and public was the actions of one of the nation's largest job placement companies. Newspaper stories had accused the company of selling franchises for $25,000 and hoping that the franchise would fail, giving the company a chance to sell another $25,000 franchise in the same locale.[4]

The staffing business was growing in the early 1960s, although the industry was still in its infancy. In 1963, the federal government reported that only 816 firms in the nation employed temporary workers. Staffing companies grossed less than $200 million in annual sales that year.

By the time Bob joined Acme Personnel, the company was more than 20 years old. It was founded in Spokane, Washington, in 1947 by David L. "Pop" Reiff, an accountant who had moved his family to Washington from Chicago after World War II. Reiff and his wife bought a small existing staffing agency in Spokane and began building the business. He made sales calls on employers while his wife, Doris, ran the office and made placements.[5]

Soon, the Reiff's son, William "Bill" Reiff, joined the company. Gordon Blair, a graduate of the University of Washington, opened Acme's third office in Seattle in 1951. Blair became the inspirational leader of the company. Two other major players in the Acme story were Tom Gunderson, who came on board in 1962, and Ralph Palmen, who joined the company in 1965 a few months before Bob.[6]

Bob's role in the Acme office was limited. He was not allowed to interview job applicants but searched through applications and attempted to match workers with jobs. Once he made a match, he handed the information to one of the counselors in the office to make the call.[7]

Bob caught on to the system quickly. Application cards were notched for particular skills. Bob ran a thin probe that resembled a knitting needle through a particular notch in a stack of cards. All the cards of workers with that skill level fell out.

Bob worked with two men and two women in the Acme office developing mostly small employer accounts. An exception to the small employer business was an arrangement to find management trainees, claims adjusters, and underwriters for the Seattle regional office of Allstate Insurance Company. Acme also filled jobs for Washington Natural Gas Company, Nedra's employer.[8]

Acme was not in the temporary placement business, but placed permanent employees. Once an employer hired one of Acme's applicants, the worker had to pay the placement fee that normally was approximately $200.

Each screener in the Acme office was required to make 15 referrals of workers to employers each day. The hope was that one permanent job would be found from the 15 referrals, giving the counselor the required 20 job placements a month. Frankly, it was difficult to get applicants to drive into downtown Seattle

A typical Acme Personnel job applicant referral card. In the early years of the personnel business, every aspect of the job was manual. The computer age was still in the future.

to apply for work. "We had to sell pretty hard to get them to come downtown, find a place to park, and come to the sixth floor of the Vance Building to apply for a job," Bob remembered.[9]

By the end of 1965, with three months experience, Bob began assuming new responsibilities. Much of the reason was that the two men in the office resigned. Reid Bailey took a job as a pharmaceutical representative. A week later, Bill Todd, became a warehouse manager. Because women were never promoted to branch manager positions in that era, Bob became office manager.[10]

Bob immediately began competing for production awards with Ralph Palmen, who at about the same time, became the manager of Acme's North Seattle office. Because Palmen's office was easier to access, he beat Bob every month but one over the next few years. As business improved, Bob's office averaged 87 placements a month, but Palmen averaged 113 a month.[11]

Bob intensified Acme's efforts to recruit job applicants. He stepped up advertising in the help wanted section of Seattle newspapers. He also began sending flyers, called casting card mailings, to employers. The flyers listed the job skills and experience of 40 to 50 applicants, identified on the flyer only by a number. When employers received a flyer, the telephone immediately began ringing. Bob's staff matched up the employee number with the person and sent the person to the interested business or provided space in the Acme office for the employer to interview the job applicant.[12]

One of the most experienced employees in the office was Viola Dand. She was considerably older than Bob and was a veteran in the staffing business. Everyone else had trouble getting along with Dand but Bob effectively used his humor to calm her down when she became upset. Bob had her "eating out of the palm of his hand" after about a year because he kidded her into submission. For example, if she said, "I am not going to do that," Bob replied, "Well, if you aren't, then your paycheck is not going to be here next week." Bob and Dand eventually became good friends.[13]

People liked to work for Bob. Ralph Palmen said, "He always had good people working for him. He treated them right and with respect." Once, Bob interviewed a potential jobs counselor but sent him to Palmen's North Seattle office because there was an immediate opening there. After Palmen interviewed the man, he said, "I don't want to work for you. I want to work for Bob Funk."[14]

Bob quickly discovered he was in the sales business. He had never anticipated being a salesman, but received a great thrill

BELOW: Bob, left, received the President's Award
from Acme Personnel President Bill Reiff in 1968.

ABOVE: Gordon Blair, left, recognizes future Express franchisee Dale Kjack during an early Acme Personnel convention.

LEFT: Acme Personnel leaders included, left to right, Bob Funk, Tom Gunderson, Gordon Larson, Bill Reiff, Eddie Clark, David L. "Pop" Reiff, and Gordon Blair.

when he matched a worker, whose family was suffering from no income, with a good-paying job. At first, Bob's bosses thought he spent too much time attending to the personal needs of the workers. If they were going through a rough time, Bob counseled them and shared his Christian testimony.

After a while, he took care of their job needs during the business week but often invited applicants to drop by the office for an informal counseling session on Saturday afternoon when the Acme office was less hectic. Bob sincerely wanted to help people find a job and direction for their lives. He would stay long after hours just to give them hope.[15]

As the nation's economy blossomed, the temporary and permanent staffing business grew. Acme developed an Executive Suite division to recruit higher-paid executives for employers. The company also maintained a license agreement with Kelly Services to provide temporary employees under the Kelly Girl and Kelly Labor names in six offices in Washington and British Columbia.[16]

After Bob was at Acme for two years, he thought about quitting the staffing business. The industry's image was negative in many circles. Counselors were called "flesh peddlers" and "body pushers." He discovered other companies were cheating potential employers by reporting higher scores on the Wonderlic evaluation test and inflating the number of words that a secretary could type.

Bob carefully considered his future. He had learned from his mentors at Acme to be honest about the skills of workers and the good and bad elements of a matched job. He knew that, for the long term, providing quality workers with quality jobs would make money.

In the end, what made Bob stay in the staffing business were the notes and calls of thanks he received from both workers and employers who appreciated the match Bob and his staff provided. It was like putting puzzles together, matching a background and experience of a particular person with an employer's need. Bob said, "It might not have been a perfect puzzle—but at least it was a fit."[17]

As Seattle's business activity changed, so did the role of Acme. By 1968, nearly one-third of Acme's business was providing light industrial warehouse shipping clerks. Seattle was a heavy distribution center. Many companies needed entry level shipping clerks and key punch operators to manage inventories.

While Bob worked for Acme, Nedra continued her job at Washington Natural Gas Company until 90 days before their first child was due—very unusual for the time. To stay closer to home, she became the Duvall Town Clerk, a part-time position in which she kept municipal records and accepted payments for sewer and water service. She worked until the day Julie Ann Funk was born in Seattle on May 2, 1968.[18]

In early 1969, Bob believed it was time to change his direction within the company. He had done well as office manager of the downtown Seattle Acme branch, but he wanted more challenges. At his own expense, he flew to Spokane to meet with Bill Reiff who had bought his father's interest in Acme Personnel. Bob asked Reiff what his future was at Acme. Reiff revealed plans to buy staffing services in Phoenix, Arizona; Fort Worth, Texas; Des Moines, Iowa; Minneapolis, Minnesota; and Oklahoma City, Oklahoma.

Reiff was aware of services in those cities in which owners of Kelly Girl franchises were approaching retirement age and might be interested in selling. The Kelly Girl part of the business was providing secretaries to employers. The Kelly Labor franchises matched applicants with light industrial jobs. At the end of their conversation, Reiff told Bob that he was a valuable asset to Acme and he would "come up with something."[19]

Six months later, in November, 1968, Reiff called Bob and asked to meet with Nedra and him at the Seattle airport the next afternoon. Reiff said Gordon Blair would also be at the meeting—so Bob knew something was up. He thought Reiff might offer him an opportunity to manage a new operation in one of the states in which Acme was planning to expand. Bob had only been through Oklahoma and Minnesota on driving trips with his mother to see family in Indiana. He had never been to Phoenix or Fort Worth, so whatever Reiff decided, Bob and Nedra would be launching into unknown territory.

At the airport meeting, Reiff gave Bob two options—head up the executive recruiting division of Acme Personnel or manage an office of a retiring staffing agency owner in Oklahoma City. The executive recruiting division job was open because Dean Little had been fired from the position because of lack of production.

Reiff thought Bob would probably take the executive recruiting division job and stay in Washington because he lived in Duvall across the street from his parents and down the street from Nedra's parents. Reiff wanted an answer before he was scheduled to return by airplane to Spokane four hours later. Bob and Nedra talked briefly and decided they were ready for a change of scenery. They chose Oklahoma City. Bob told Reiff, "This is an opportunity for me to strike out on my own and be that entrepreneur I wanted to be—and I can do it on your money!"[20]

In the back of his mind, Bob thought, "If I don't succeed in Oklahoma, I can always come back to Seattle in a couple of years and go to work for Boeing and make twice the money I'm making."[21]

Bob and Nedra knew nothing about Oklahoma but wanted a fresh start with their seven-month-old baby girl, Julie. They went home, told their parents about their plans, and began preparing to move halfway across North America.

Bob was appointed
to a seat on the
**Piedmont Board of
Education in 1975.**
*Courtesy Oklahoma
Publishing Company.*

Nine

MY KIND OF COUNTRY

BEFORE BOB AND NEDRA MOVED to Oklahoma, Bill Reiff and Bob flew to Oklahoma City to meet Esther Brindley, a kind lady who ran a Kelly Girl franchise in the City National Bank Building at Robinson and Robert S. Kerr avenues. On a cold, blustery Oklahoma winter day, they looked over the office and met the four employees who worked for Brindley. That night they stayed at the Skirvin Hotel down the street.[1]

The most veteran employee was Ruby Brannon, who had worked in the job placement business for 16 years. Another long-time employee was Ann Steiger. However, Bob did not fear supervising older, more experienced employees, because of his time overseeing the work of Viola Dand in Seattle.

Bob returned to Duvall and helped Nedra pack their belongings. They shipped their piano and small belongings and headed cross country to Oklahoma City. When they arrived they rented an apartment at Northeast 29th Street and Stiles Avenue.[2]

Bob took Nedra and Julie downtown to see the staffing agency. They could not believe how friendly Oklahomans were. Strangers stopped them on the street and asked about Julie. While on the elevator in the City National Bank building, more strangers asked about the baby. Bob remembered, "In Seattle, no one would have paid attention to us. In Oklahoma, complete strangers treated us like longtime friends. They even asked how old Julie was and if she was teething."[3]

When the Funks walked into the staffing agency, Esther Brindley, the owner, took an immediate liking to the young family. Brindley remembered, "They were just clean cut kids with a beautiful baby. I wanted to sell my business to someone who would keep finding jobs for Oklahomans—and I knew Bob was the right man."[4]

Brindley had started Brindley Personnel 20 years before and had a good reputation for providing secretaries for downtown law firms and other businesses. A former Major in the United States Army Women's Auxiliary Corps during World War II, Brindley was a sharp businesswoman.[5]

While Brindley kept managing the temporary placement business under the Kelly Girls banner, Bob took over her business of matching applicants with permanent employment positions under the name Acme-Brindley Personnel Service. Acme decided to keep Brindley's name in the official name of the company because of her stellar reputation. Acme promised in its contract with Brindley to not compete for temporary staffing business for five years.[6]

Bob oversaw remodeling of his new office and began to familiarize himself with the Oklahoma City business community, especially clients who had used Brindley Personnel to fill jobs. Mrs. Brindley became like a grandmother to the Funks. She introduced Bob to many of the area's civic clubs and the chamber of commerce.

Ralph Palmen came to Oklahoma City and taught Bob how to successfully recruit executives for higher paying positions. He took Bob on his first sales call to Macklanburg-Duncan, a major Oklahoma City manufacturing company.[7]

On Sundays, Bob, Nedra, and Julie drove around the city and the surrounding countryside. Bob could not believe that farm and ranch land lay just beyond Baptist Hospital on the northwest side. The drives into the countryside reminded him of his rural upbringing in Duvall.[8]

In the office, Bob made friends with his employees and began building the business. His leadership style was completely different than Miss Brindley. Bob was softer and employed a more motivational management style. He said, "That appealed to the workers. They really dug in and wanted to help me be successful in the business."[9]

Nedra helped organize the office for Bob, then took a full-time job as a customer service supervisor at Fidelity National Bank in downtown Oklahoma City. She left Julie with babysitters who lived in the same apartment complex.

After six months in the apartment, Bob and Nedra bought a home on 24 acres in Piedmont, a community northwest of the Oklahoma City metropolitan area. Piedmont was near the geographical center of Oklahoma in Canadian County. The Funks moved into an old house at 506 Piedmont Road, in the heart of the business district of the town.

Piedmont was born in the famous Oklahoma Land Run on April 22, 1889. James Dean, no relation to the actor or sausage king, rode his horse from the starting line to the 160 acres he homesteaded. After his death a decade later, a medical doctor and attorney, E.H. Long, bought the property and had a townsite laid out. Piedmont officially became a town in 1903.[10]

With the coming of the St. Louis-El Reno-Western Railroad in 1904, Piedmont began to flourish. Lots along the railroad right-of-way were auctioned and settlers in nearby rural areas flocked to the town. In 1905, a two-story, four-room school was built. A year later, the first telephone service was installed.

Oklahoma became a state in 1907 and Piedmont was incorporated in 1909. The lifeblood of early Piedmont business was agriculture, especially wheat production.[11]

Even though a fire in 1932 destroyed much of Piedmont's business district, the town survived and its population had doubled by 1970 when the Funks arrived. It was still a friendly, small village. Nedra said, "It reminded us of Duvall. Everyone knew everyone else, and we looked out for each other's interest."[12]

Bob's first year in Oklahoma was successful. He showed a loss of about $20,000, but most of that was attributable to start-up costs. New clients were added and Bob moved Ann Steiger into a branch office in a small shopping center at Northwest 50th Street and May Avenue in northwest Oklahoma City.

Just as the two offices were showing a profit, a recession reduced business expansion and cut into the job placements Bob's offices were showing. The Arab oil embargo caused gasoline prices to soar and the American economy suffered greatly. Bob cut his overhead and Acme officials borrowed money to keep the offices open.

In the beginning, Bill Reiff made the move to Oklahoma City financially attractive to Bob. He promised him a decent salary and said he would eventually receive 50 percent of the profits of the Oklahoma operation. It was great motivation to make the operation profitable, and Bob did.[13]

By 1971, Acme Personnel was the largest staffing agency in the world owned by one individual. To celebrate the growth and provide additional incentive to Bob, Reiff gave him a new title—vice president of operations in Texas, Oklahoma, Iowa, Minnesota, Arkansas, and Colorado. Bob traveled to Acme offices in those states and made lifetime friendships with franchise owners.

An example is Mark and Sheryl Tasler, who bought a failing Acme office in Rochester, Minnesota, after visiting with a college friend in South Dakota who operated an Acme office.[14]

The Taslers were fresh out of college and knew nothing about the personnel business. They also did not know a single person in Rochester. But after four days of training, they opened for business and made money their second month.[15]

As in other states, the faltering economy made business in Minnesota tough. Most of the workload was handling placements for clerical, light industrial, bookkeeping, accounting, and computer programming. The computer age had just arrived and companies were looking for people with enough technical skill to at least turn on a computer.[16]

Bob took great care to teach his employees and franchisees what he knew about the staffing business. He taught the Taslers that growth happened when they learned something and duplicated the process. They were told to never be afraid of takings risks, to love their employees, family, and friends, and to never stop learning. Bob also preached the idea that all should give back more than they take from society and that business leaders should not be afraid to express their faith and love for God.[17]

Today, the Taslers lead several very successful Express Personnel offices and have been major contributors to the company's success.

In 1972, Acme celebrated its 25th anniversary. The company had placed 250,000 people in jobs in the United States and Canada. A corporate staff of 125 people oversaw 71 office locations. Thirty-one of the offices were owned by the company and the remaining stores were franchise operations.[18]

In 1973, William H. "Bill" Stoller joined Acme as a part-time employee at an office in Portland, Oregon, after being

BOB FUNK...

.... the **"IN"** candidate

for

Piedmont Board of Education

recruited by Tom Gunderson. Stoller was a college basketball player who impressed his superiors. Stoller liked the competitive environment of the staffing business. It was like sports and was fun for him because he was dealing with people.[19]

One of the ways Bob attracted new clients to the agency was by placing advertisements that looked like special correspondent columns in *The Daily Oklahoman.* The ad, titled, "The Advantages of Using a Private Employment Agency," appeared with Bob's photograph and identified him as an officer of Acme Personnel Services. In part, the ad said, "People who have found employment through the services of a private employment agency are frequently quick to recommend to their friends the efficiency of job-seeking with the help of a good agency."[20] The ad, a new and innovative advertising method, also invited readers to look at the Acme job listings in the newspaper's classified ads.

Even with the successful advertising, circumstances beyond Bob's control hurt his business. The recession and gas shortage in 1974 and 1975 severely limited the growth of job placement services across the nation. Business at Acme dropped 25 percent in 1975 at the company's 84 offices in 16 states and Canada.

There was no drop in activity at the Funk household. Nedra gave birth to Robert Allen "Bobby" Funk, Jr., at Deaconess Hospital in Oklahoma City on May 5, 1975. After Nedra had worked as supervisor of customer accounts for Fidelity National Bank, she did accounting for Sav-Go, an automobile service station business, and started a gift shop, Country Treasures, in Piedmont.[21]

Bob became active in community affairs. He was appointed to the Piedmont Board of Education. At the time, Piedmont High School offered only 17 core subjects. Bob wanted to serve on the school board to help the children of his community and also to counter a smear campaign that was being conducted against the school superintendent, David R. Owens. Bob believed in the forward-thinking ideas of Owens. When anonymous letters were sent to parents and school board members alleging Owens had used school equipment to work on his home, Bob defended him, telling a newspaper reporter, "Whoever is doing this is sick!"[22]

Bob was reelected to five-year terms on the school board in 1976 and 1981. During that time, he led the fight to establish high school and elementary counseling programs; to strengthen school discipline; to initiate a policy of 20 credits for graduation; to start tennis, track, and FFA programs; to greatly increase the number of core subjects; and to complete construction of a student lounge and auditorium.[23]

In 1976, largely because Bob heard negative and untrue information being circulated in the community about the school superintendent, Bob and Jim Martin founded Piedmont's first newspaper, the *Piedmont-Surrey Gazette*. Bob wanted the newspaper to tell the truth about community news. Martin had been a human resources director at Sequoyah Mills but came to work for Bob in Oklahoma City as an executive recruiter. Martin had experience in the newspaper business and was a perfect partner for Bob.

As in other Bob Funk ventures, Nedra was called into action. She and Martin's wife, Laura, sold advertisements, laid out the paper, and had it printed each week.

Religion continued to be a major part of the Funks' life. They attended First Baptist Church of Piedmont and enjoyed the preaching of Pastor R.B. Mathis. The only problem Bob encountered at the new church was the rule that he must be baptized again to become a member. For years, Bob did not join the church because he had been baptized in the ultimate place, the Jordan River, where Jesus was baptized by John the Baptist. Bob was leading singing and teaching a Sunday School class at the church and thought he should be grandfathered-in on the baptism requirement. Finally, he gave in and was baptized again.[24]

ABOVE: The Funks in 1976. Left to right, Bob, Nedra, Bobby, and Julie.

LEFT: Left to right, Roy Funk, Bob, and Joanne Funk Benton in 1979.

Bob became good friends with Reverend Mathis. Bob owned a small John Deere tractor which he used to mow his yard. First Baptist did not own a lawnmower so Bob loaned his tractor to the pastor each week to mow the yard at the church and the pastor's home.

"Bob would give the shirt off his back for anyone in need," Reverend Mathis said, "On more than one occasion he shared his good fortune with my family and others in the community who were in need."[25]

Nedra stayed busy. She had her hands full raising two children but always was involved in other adventures. For seven years, she operated a very successful daycare center at First

Baptist Church in Piedmont. She also managed a tag agency in Piedmont until many of the responsibilities of the office went to Bob's niece, Terri Weldon.

Later, Bob convinced Nedra to take over the bookkeeping and accounting work for the fledgling company. He promised it would only take two or three days a week, but the growing company soon required more than 40 hours a week of Nedra's time.

Bob became the official tag agent in Piedmont in 1984. Nedra ran the office until many of the duties were taken over by their niece, Terri Weldon, shown in this photograph demonstrating use of the camera for making drivers licenses. *Courtesy Oklahoma Publishing Company.*

LEFT: Julie, eating corn on the cob, at her grandmother's house.

BELOW: Bobby was born May 5, 1975, in Oklahoma City. This is his first grade picture.

Meanwhile, Bob was doing everything he could to increase sales. He decided that marketing and sales could fuel growth in his operation. He hired Art Atkinson, Susan Mullanix, and Sandra VanZant to implement his new strategy of hiring more sales-oriented people to contact companies directly, rather than depend upon more passive marketing techniques such as mailings, giveaways, and press releases. Atkinson, Mullanix, and VanZant are still with Bob in major leadership roles in Express Personnel Services.[26]

The first year of using the new strategy resulted in a $40,000 loss. It took a lot of money to hire good sales people. Also, the three recessions in the 1970s hurt the permanent job placement business. It was obvious to Bob that temporary "temp" staffing was the new game in town. Several of the major Acme franchisees

Attending a meeting of the National Association of Temporary Services were, left to right, front row, Bob, Nedra, and Susan Mullanix. Standing, third and fourth from the left are Jim and Carol Gray.

around the country created their own temporary staffing companies.[27]

One franchisee, Jim Gray, formed his own temp company in Boulder, Colorado. Dorothy Van Treeck in Gray's office designed a payroll system that worked well in the temp business. The system was sold to several Acme operators. Expansion was on the horizon. Bob, Gray, and Bill Stoller were asked to start Andex Temporary Help, a subsidiary of Acme, to provide a framework for a nationwide temporary staffing business.[28]

In Oklahoma, as the temp business grew, workers in Bob's offices used a Selectric typewriter to type hundreds of weekly payroll checks.

A healthy change in the way of doing business in Bob's Oklahoma offices was the trend of employers, rather than the workers, paying the placement fees. It created a much more stable flow of income and Bob's office managers no longer had to depend upon having to discount a note from a worker to a credit company. Another problem with the old system was that workers who quit early did not pay their fees and Acme workers' commission checks were reduced. Local managers spent much of their time in small claims court attempting to collect unpaid applicant fees.[29]

Bob began taking care of the many details involved in running a successful operation. He insisted on his job counselors answering the telephone correctly. Sandra VanZant, who ran the Acme Personnel office in Shawnee, Oklahoma, remembered, "There was an exact script to follow and I was terrified of doing it wrong."[30] Bob often visited his branch offices to help, especially during times of heavy applicant intake. VanZant recalled a time when Bob sat at a desk in the back of the office and interviewed more than 40 people.[31]

Bob's Acme operation attracted quality workers largely because of Bob's reputation of being fair to his employees. In 1979, Carol Lane reentered the workforce after several years as a stay-at-home mom. When she interviewed with Bob, she was immediately impressed, "After meeting with him, I knew he was someone I could trust because he had a quality about him that made me feel at ease. I considered him to be a very professional and intelligent man and someone I knew I could work with on a daily basis."[32] Lane handled billing and applicant testing at the north Oklahoma City Acme office. Today, she still serves as Bob's right hand. She said, "27 years later, I still see a new, energized Bob Funk every day. He truly walks his talk."[33]

By the late 1970s, the temporary staffing business in America had become one of the nation's fastest growing service industries. Industry sales in 1978 topped $2 billion, compared to $160 million 15 years before. In 1963, very few American workers were temporaries. But by 1978, temporaries comprised three percent of the total work force. There were more than two million temporary workers on the payroll of American businesses.[34]

Acme had 84 offices in 22 states and Andex, Acme's subsidiary, had opened 25 offices in just one year. The leading national staffing companies, Kelly and Olsten, held 30 percent of the market of the temporary business. Andex was one of only two large temp services west of the Mississippi River.[35]

The temporary help business attracted employers because they escaped the time and expense of recruiting and hiring employees, especially for short-term or seasonal assignments. It also provided professional, full-time recruiters to aid in hiring and eliminated the lead time of getting "staffed up" for a project. Employers soon learned they could avoid unemployment costs when employees were let go at the end of the season or project.

Employees learned they benefited as well, because they had a personal employment "agent" helping them find a new job when the old assignment ran out or finding them a better job when their skills and experience increased. Temporary staffing lessened what economists refer to as "frictional unemployment," the amount of time an employee has between jobs.

"Just-in-time" inventory of labor was born. Employers benefited from an overall reduction in labor costs. The key was that temporary staffing provided only the amount of labor needed, when it was needed.[36]

The changing landscape of the staffing industry caused great financial stress on Acme Personnel. Bob knew for years that cash flow was a problem for Bill Reiff. At one point, Reiff was more than $70,000 behind in paying Bob his share of the profits from the Oklahoma operation. Bob often had arguments with the corporate office when he received monthly statements. Almost every month, expenses from some other operation or corporate travel expenses were deducted from Bob's account.[37]

Reiff had repaid most of the $200,000 he borrowed to see Acme through early recessions, but those loans were nothing compared to the money he had to borrow during the recession in 1981 and 1982. While Bob was opening new Acme offices in Little Rock, Arkansas, and Houston and Fort Worth, Texas, Reiff borrowed nearly $1 million from Employer's Credit Corporation, and could not repay the loan. Reiff was having a tough time keeping his companies solvent.[38]

In fact, Bob's Acme offices in Oklahoma were supporting operations that were losing money in other states. Reiff asked his franchisees to put money into his credit corporation to make the entire company structure stronger. Bob refused—primarily because he did not have any extra money to invest in the venture.[39]

Bob also became concerned about Reiff's health. When Reiff addressed an Oklahoma City Rotary Club meeting in May, 1982, his speech was slurred, and he missed punch lines to jokes and did not complete ideas. Reiff was an excellent speaker, and Bob could tell something was wrong. Bob was right. Reiff was diagnosed with a brain tumor the next week.[40]

Bob's employees were unaware of the financial problems of the parent company. New counselors were given training and information manuals to read. Within days of being hired, they marketed in the morning and interviewed and filled job orders each afternoon. Ruby Brannon, the veteran "placement queen" was joined by young people like Jerry Magee and

Cindy Fairchild. After working as a real estate agent, Fairchild took on the challenge at the permanent placement desk at Acme.

She remembered, "Art Atkinson and I were 'missionary-driven' about our applicants and wanted to save the world and place everyone in better working conditions." One day Fairchild was so concerned about the plight of one of her applicants, she asked Art to pray with the man in his office. After a few minutes, the man regained his composure, and Fairchild continued the interview.[41]

By 1982, the recession had caused a drop in the temporary employee business, and Acme was experiencing serious financial difficulties. Reiff had borrowed all the money he could and was fighting the brain tumor just to stay alive. With his death imminent, his son, Steve, entered the business to try to keep it afloat. If asked, Bob would have done anything to help save the company. His territory was the most profitable in the company, and he felt responsible for keeping Acme together.

Bob, Tom Gunderson, Gordon Larson, and Gordon Blair were still loyal to Reiff and would have signed $250,000 notes to keep the company running. Even though they were owed money, the longtime Acme managers appreciated the opportunity Reiff had given them in the past. But Steve Reiff had other ideas.[42]

Steve began trying to raise capital by selling franchises to the managers of Acme's own corporate offices. Gordon Blair was not interested—so he was fired. So was Tom Gunderson. Steve Reiff wanted to fire Bob, but he saw Bob's successful operation as a way to raise capital. He valued the Oklahoma operation at $550,000. If he could get that kind of money from Bob, it would repay almost half the Acme corporate debt. But Bob did not have $5,000—let alone $550,000.[43]

Julie was an excellent student in elementary school at Piedmont.

Bob believed it was time to share the Acme problems with his management team. He gathered everyone and outlined his options. Steve Reiff was making it easy for Bob to decide to launch out with his own company. The mood of his managers was unanimous. Sandra VanZant said, "Bob, wherever you go on Monday morning is where we will be!"

Bob wanted to buy his five offices. He was a risk-taker and "had enough faith in his people" that he knew he could make the staffing business work. He tried to borrow the money to meet Reiff's price, but was turned down by every banker to whom he talked. Finally, an agreement was reached, although last minute problems almost spoiled the deal.

Ten

OUT OF THE ASHES

BOB WORKED OUT THE TEDIOUS DETAILS of his purchase of the Oklahoma Acme operations with Bill Reiff, whose condition was quickly deteriorating, and with Reiff's son, Steve. Bob, who had worked closely with the elder Reiff for his entire career in the staffing industry, was devastated by Reiff's terminal illness. Ralph Palmen began calling Bob on a regular basis to try and lift his spirits.[1]

A matter that complicated negotiations was that Reiff still owed Bob $72,000 in past bonuses. Another hang up was Steve Reiff's insistence that Bob buy both the permanent and temporary sides of the Oklahoma Acme operation. Bob only wanted to purchase the permanent part of the business. He did not see the need to pay for the temporary business because he had never had a non-compete provision with Acme on temporary hires. The expert leader was dying.[2]

On December 21, 1982, documents were signed that gave Bob the Acme Personnel Service business with offices in Tulsa, Del City, Norman, Shawnee, and two locations in Oklahoma City—an office at Southwest 74th Street and Pennsylvania

LEFT: An early advertising flyer for Express Temporary Service.

A copy of the check that Bob used to purchase
Acme Personnel's offices in Oklahoma in 1982.

Avenue and the location where Bob officed at 4334 Northwest
Expressway.[3]

The total sales price for the business and offices was
$235,000. The Reiffs wanted a $75,000 down payment. Bob
agreed to forgive half of what the Reiffs owed him in bonuses
and apply the other half to the down payment. However, he still
had to come up with the balance. Bob visited with loan officers
at several large Oklahoma City banks without success.

He then borrowed the money from Rolling Hills State Bank
in Piedmont, using his home and property as collateral. Bob and
Nedra formed Oklahoma Personnel Service, Inc. to operate the
new permanent employment agency business.[4]

The Funks created a new corporation, Oklahoma Temporary
Service, Inc., to handle the temporary part of the business. They
also started a company called Apex Temporary Service with the
help of Susan Mullinax and Ginny Kidwell. The Apex operation was profitable from the beginning. In its first six months
of business, Apex recorded sales of $846,591 and showed a net
profit of $93,778. The cash flow allowed Bob some latitude in
determining his own future.[5]

Even with Bob owning the former Oklahoma Acme Personnel
operation, his new position was clouded by Acme's problems.

Bill Reiff died in February, 1983. Mortgages that Reiff had negotiated before his death effectively blocked Bob's right of first refusal to buy the entire company, an option he had negotiated for in the purchase agreement with Acme.[6]

Acme Personnel began crumbling. Offices around the country closed, and Bob's staff found themselves unemployed. Often, workers received the word by a phone call from the corporate office, "It's over. Close the office." No one knew what to do with files or office furniture. They just left.[7]

In the back of his mind, Bob, being part of the Acme inner circle, believed he still might save the company. But every day he discovered new financial problems or other liens placed against the stock of Acme and Andex, the temporary side of Acme's business. Instead of trying to salvage the old company, Bob moved in a different direction—he wanted to form a new company.[8]

He called Bill Stoller and Jim Gray in March, 1983, and explored the possibility of the three men forming a new corporation, to leave behind the blight of complicated financial dealings of Acme. The three were moving rapidly toward creating the new company when they arrived at Acme's annual meeting in Boulder, Colorado, in April. However, as they checked into the hotel, they received a letter stating that Steve Reiff had placed Acme in bankruptcy.

Bob, Stoller, and Gray already had decided they would have a booth at the convention advertising their new staffing company. With the news of the Acme bankruptcy, they went a step further. At a general meeting at the convention, they presented their plan of forming a new company to employees from 52 of the 84 Acme offices that remained open.[9]

An outspoken Acme franchisee at the general meetings was Dale Kjack of Cheyenne, Wyoming. Initially, Kjack was against

RIGHT: The three founders of Express Temporary Help Service, later renamed Express Services, Inc., left to right, James R. "Jim" Gray, Bob Funk, and William H. "Bill" Stoller.

ABOVE: Bob, center, gives an award to Ralph Palmen, left, and Darlys Palmen. Bob originally worked with Ralph at Acme Personnel in Seattle.

BELOW: Bob, his father, and sister, at niece Jodi Benton's wedding in 1983. Left to right, Roy Funk, Joanne Funk Benton, and Bob.

the new company. He still was smarting from the disastrous results of the failure of Acme and finger-pointing at Reiff. Kjack said, "We don't want one leader of a company any more." Bob's response was, "We've got three leaders of this company."[10]

After the Acme meeting, several events solidified the efforts of Bob, Stoller, and Gray to go forward with their new company. No one wanted to sue Acme for any of the wrongs the company had committed. Bob decided to hang on to his Acme permanent operation and let things take their course. Stoller decided to go with the new company—Express—but when he returned from vacation, the holder of one of Reiff's many mortgages, had taken Stoller's business records and employees.[11]

Bob, Stoller, and Gray scraped together enough money to have a lawyer draft documents creating Express Temporary Help Service, Inc. The name "Express" was actually third on the founders' original list. Other names they had discussed for the new company were FlexForce and Excel, but those names already were taken.[12]

Bob unveiled his plans to his employees and told them that the next few years might be difficult. He asked people like Art Atkinson to take on the responsibility of three jobs—train new people, supervise an office, and see clients. Bob also asked his workers to chip in some money to buy stock in the new company. At first, Atkinson told Bob, "I make $550 a month. Do you think I have anything left over to chip into the pot?" But Atkinson believed in Bob and the new company and "scraped up every dime he could" to invest in Express.[13]

There were still battles with Steve Reiff who was trying to salvage Acme from bankruptcy. At one point, he threatened to come to Oklahoma City and take over Bob's Acme offices. Bob stood his ground and said, "You can come, but you'll find all the offices empty. My managers are loyal to me."[14]

Express Temporary Help Service started with eight offices—Bob's five Oklahoma locations, Stoller's office in Oregon, and Gray's two locations in Colorado. The talents and skills of the three founders blended perfectly. Gray managed payroll and bookkeeping operations in the Boulder, Colorado office. Bob and Stoller were the salesmen, selling licenses, and later franchises, to personnel agencies across the country.[15]

Bob's employees in Oklahoma grappled with the unknown—what lay ahead for the company operating under a new name? Susan Mullanix originally did not like the name Express because

Bob at his desk in August, 1983. He had just been interviewed by a reporter from *The Daily Oklahoman* about the status of the economy and the recession's effect on the staffing industry. *Courtesy Oklahoma Publishing Company.*

Early Express Personnel management included, left to right, front row, Ralph Palmen, Nell Pinson, and Mark Tasler. Standing, Bob Funk, Chris Corrigan, Jerry Scofield, and Tom Gunderson.

she was afraid of losing clients by changing names again. She said, "Was I wrong! We were Andex one day, Apex the next, and then Express. Our clients did not have a problem with that because they were connected to us personally."[16]

The new company had its first board meeting in June, 1983. Bob was elected president, Stoller was named vice president, and Gray became secretary-treasurer. Each founder received 26,000 shares of the 100,000 shares authorized by the articles of incorporation. Other shareholders included Gray's wife, Carol, Ralph Palmen, Peyton Rice, Susan Mullanix, Michael Egan, Nell Pinson, and Magee Enterprises, Inc.

The board passed a resolution designating Boulder as the national headquarters. Income from Bob's five offices in

Oklahoma supplied much of the revenue for the overhead of the new national company. Most of the corporate functions, except for payroll, were handled by Bob's employees in Oklahoma.

From its birth, the founders of Express wanted to expand to 84 offices within three years because that had been the size of Acme before its demise. That goal was accomplished in three years and ten months.

The growth of Express was so costly that Bob could not always generate enough income to make payroll. In lieu of cash, he paid early team members in shares of stock. For each day spent in the field or training, employees received 100 shares of stock. Even with the barter form of payment, Bob still had to borrow $150,000 to keep the company solvent.[17]

The efforts of the new company paid off. Within a few weeks of the formation of the new company, offices in Little Rock and Fort Smith, Arkansas, and Greeley, Colorado, joined Express. All were former Acme franchises. The Fort Smith office was owned by Jerry and Paul Magee. Peyton Rice owned the Little Rock office, and Kathy and Mike Egan owned the Greeley office. Before the end of 1983, Dellamae Henkle opened an Express office in Medford, Oregon, and Ralph and Darlys Palmen joined Express with their office in Lynnwood, Washington.[18]

In August, 1983, Tom Gunderson moved to Oklahoma City to help Bob build the company. He began working as an executive recruiter and began selling licenses for new offices. However, he was so unsure of the future of the company, he told his parents he would be back home in Oregon by spring.[19]

Staffing service veterans such as Ralph Palmen believed Bob could lead the new organization to be even greater than Acme. He saw differences between the leadership styles of Bob and Bill Reiff. Palmen said, "Bob was better at listening to other people, in bringing in consultants like Ed Peppin, who had expertise in areas unknown to Bob and the other founders."[20]

According to Palmen, Bob's strength was that he did not assume he had all the answers. Bob listened to suggestions from others who had more information. Palmen also recognized Bob's extreme loyalty to his employees, loyalty that was returned without fail. He said, "Bob's ability to empathize with others and make them feel like he really cared about their problems and their personal lives set him far above other leaders in the staffing world."[21]

Bob's managers knew that his life had always been about other people and that money was very far down the ladder of priorities. However, he needed to operate his business and keep helping people. Bob spent much of his time establishing banking relationships to operate the business for the short term.

Bob and the other Express founders agreed not to take any money out of the corporation for the first three years. Instead, they wanted all profits to be used to develop the infrastructure of the company. Actually, Bob, Stoller, and Gray were not paid by the corporation during its first five years. They paid themselves from their individual office operations.[22]

Early employees of Express also were asked to make sacrifices. They often worked into the night to complete their assignments. Operations were still primarily manual. Three forms were required to be sent to Boulder for payroll. Handwritten lists were made in the local office, and then payroll information was communicated by phone to Boulder where the payroll checks were issued.[23]

Everyone was willing to help everyone else. If there were problems in Arkansas or Colorado, Oklahoma employees went there to help, and vice versa. There was a unique camaraderie between Bob and his employees. They felt his loyalty was one of his strongest characteristics. That loyalty allowed Bob to build an organization in which co-workers such as Ralph Palmen, Terri Weldon, Sandra VanZant, Cindy Fairchild, Susan Mullinax, Art Atkinson, and Carol Lane would remain in positions of importance for decades.

There also was competitive give and take. Jerry Baird related an example:

> The girls in our office got really good at figuring what their hours [production of hours worked by temporary employees] were going to be the next week, so they'd call Bob and say, "Bob, we're going to hit 5,000 hours next week." He'd say, "No you're not!" They'd ask, "What'll you give us if we do?"

One time they wanted a microwave and they wanted him to deliver it. Of course they hit the goal, and here came Bob toting a microwave. That's the way it worked.[24]

Carol Gray, Jim Gray's wife, started an internal newsletter, *Expressions*, during the first few months of the life of the company. The in-house publication discussed the latest trends in

In 1985, Express Personnel had its first sales blitz. Left to right, National Training Director Lois Montgomery, an official of the Springdale, Arkansas, chamber of commerce, Tom Gunderson, Bill Stoller, another official, franchisee Jerry Magee Baird, Bob Funk, and Nikki Sells, manager of the Springdale office.

Bob and Joanne had a 1930 Model-A truck restored for their father for his 80th birthday in 1987. Roy earlier had owned a similar vehicle.

the industry, announced training sessions, and gave employees helpful marketing tools. *Expressions* also related success stories of placements and announced results of contests that kept employees of different offices in a competitive mood.

At the March, 1984 Express board meeting, Carol Gray was appointed communications director, Nancy Topliff became operations manager, Tom Gunderson was director of licensing, Lois Montgomery was training director, and Susan Mullanix was marketing director.[25]

Ralph Palmen began writing a training manual for the expected growth in employees. Nikki Sells, now the Express Vice President of Franchising, was a typical new employee at Jerry Baird's office in Fort Smith, Arkansas. She remembered, "We developed a procedure as we went. We were motivated by Bob's great desire to help people. Even though we possibly were rough around the edges in our approach, we knew that we wanted to go in and staff companies. We just had to go sell. It was all about sales calls and doing what we told the employers we would do. We were convinced that Bob and the company would be successful because of his intense integrity."[26]

Bob noticed a change in the temporary placement business. In the final years of Acme, more than 90 percent of placements had been clerical. By end of the first year of the Express operation, clerical placements were down 20 percent with a rise in technical, professional, and medical placements.[27]

"We began to make huge inroads with the concept of flexible staffing," Nikki Sells said. "We asked employers if they had peaks and valleys in their business." When the employers complained of the problems and exorbitant costs associated with hiring and laying off permanent employees, Sells and other Express representatives presented the advantages of temporary staffing.[28]

Several of the Express offices saw huge gains in business by mid-1984. Twenty-Nine people attended the first annual convention at the Granada Royale Hotel in Scottsdale, Arizona, in May, 1984. Bob told those in attendance at the convention that Express would provide more and better marketing tools in the near future. He also announced that the long-range goal of Express was to rank among the largest employment services in the United States by 1988.

Express was up and running.

Three generations of the Funk family.
Left to right, Bobby, Roy, and Bob.

The Funks in 1986. Bob, Nedra, Julie, and Bobby.

Eleven

THRIVING AGAIN

A WISE MAN ONCE SAID that "timing is everything." However, the unique success story of Express Personnel defied the logic of that ancient proverb. Bob had built his Acme business during unprecedented growth years in the Oklahoma economy. Oil and gas were being produced all over the state as Mercedes-Benz and Rolls-Royce dealers and expensive jewelry stores broke sales records. Unfortunately, the bottom fell out of the energy market in 1983, just as Bob was trying to get Express off the ground.

A sustained drop in energy prices, with resulting bankruptcies in the petroleum and contract drilling industries, caused Penn Square Bank in Oklahoma City to fail. In domino fashion, larger banks that had been too quick to fund any and all oil and gas drilling ventures failed. Never had the failure of one bank in one state caused so much damage to the national banking system and the national economy in general.[1]

Oklahoma's economy slipped further into recession because of falling cattle prices. The state's governor, George Nigh, had to use his bully pulpit to convince citizens and legislators to tighten their belts. The falling oil prices cut state revenues by millions of dollars each month.[2]

Somehow, Bob and Express defied the odds. All around him, many other businesses in Oklahoma failed during the severe recession in 1983 and 1984. Oklahoma was not alone in experiencing a bad economy. *U.S. News and World Report* in May, 1983, reported that 38 states had cut spending in fiscal year 1983 and several more states were headed in the same direction. Bob thought, "What a time to start a national business that is largely based upon other companies adding employees, both temporary and permanent!"[3]

There were two reasons Express succeeded during the recession—having quality people on board and a new sales concept. Because of all that happened to the economy in Oklahoma City, Bob was able to bring in experts from many important disciplines—people such as Tom Richards, Gean Atkinson, Dale Mitchell, Dave Gillogly, Linda Haneborg, Richard Roby, and Cindy Fairchild. Bob said, "It was our people who made a difference. When they saw the economy going south, they said, 'If every personnel company goes under, we'll be the last one!'"[4]

The sales concept that set Express apart from its competition was called "probationary hiring." Bob had heard of the concept at national meetings of staffing organizations. Employers had laid off workers and were reluctant to hire new permanent employees even as the economy improved. Many medium and large companies had costly benefit packages they had to offer to permanent workers.

Instead of filling new permanent positions, employers had the attractive option of allowing Express workers to assume positions in plants and businesses without having a permanent payroll. It was a win-win situation for both employer and worker. Bob said, "It gave companies confidence. If their business did not support the new workers, they did not have to fire them. If a company ran out of work, we simply moved the worker to a new company." In addition, companies did not have to be concerned about the cost of litigation that sometimes arises from firing permanent workers.[5]

Employees also benefited by being able to screen employers. Often, after a second or third assignment, a worker was hired permanently by one of the previous companies at which he or she was assigned by Express on a temporary basis.[6]

In 1984, Bob, Stoller, and Gray paid $75,000 for the bankrupt assets of Acme International and acquired the franchise rights to 30 Acme offices across the nation. Meanwhile, the Oklahoma City office led the company in best volume of production in 1984, although a major production award was won by Hank Eidenmuller of Corpus Christi, Texas. Eidenmuller had been the first non-Acme franchisee to join Express. In 2007, he was still a vibrant contributor to the company and was the recipient of the highest award Express offers—the Gordon Blair Award.[7]

The marketing and promotion programs made Express unique among staffing services. For the Labor Day promotion in 1984, Express staff wore hard hats printed with the Express logo and delivered gourmet brown bag lunches to major industrial clients. The lunch bags were printed with a "weepul," a cute, fuzzy cartoon creature wearing a white hard hat with a ribbon bearing the Express logo. The weepul, a popular idea with clients, appeared in future Express promotions.[8]

In the early years of Express, Bob spent much of his time on the road. He and others visited former Acme Personnel franchisees with promises that Express could increase their business by 40 percent by using marketing methods the new company had perfected. Bob put his reputation on the line to convince Mark Tasler that he could increase his weekly production from 800 to

1,120 hours. By the end of the year after Tasler officially became part of Express, he was billing 2,800 hours a week.[9]

Soon after Express Temporary Help Services began business, the name "Help" was dropped from all stationery and advertisements. In 1985, the corporate name was changed to Express Services, Inc.

In April, 1985, Express spent $80,000 and installed a state-of-the-art computer system in Boulder. The new system allowed franchisees to key in employee, client, job, and time card information from remote locations. The new system replaced occasional all-night sessions at offices around the country.[10]

New Express offices sprang up all over the nation. The growth of the company allowed Bob to hire former banker, Dale Mitchell, as the company's first chief operating officer. Mitchell helped Bob, Stoller, and Gray identify areas of banking concerns of future growth.

The company was literally outgrowing its banking connections in Boulder and Oklahoma City. With increased weekly temporary payrolls, the company needed larger loans, something the smaller banks they had dealt with were unable to complete.

In Oklahoma, Ralph Farrar became Bob's personal banker and close friend. On Saturday mornings, Bob would drop by the bank to cash a check and then sit for long conversations with Farrar. "Bob is a warm and generous man," Farrar said, "He would help anyone in need and go out of his way to do so." Farrar remembered the occasion when Bob bought a scoreboard for Piedmont High School's football stadium just because he wanted the school to have it and because he was a good citizen of the school district.[11]

On one Sunday afternoon at a western art auction, having his banker along was beneficial to Bob. He found some pieces

Express employees and franchisees always had great conventions. Here, Bob and Nedra, in wigs and letter sweaters, participate in a '50s fun night at the 1988 convention in Portland, Oregon.

of art he wanted to buy but he had forgotten his checkbook. Farrar paid for the purchases with his own check. Bob, of course, was at the bank on Monday morning with a check in hand to repay Farrar.[12]

The cost of workers' compensation became a major concern for the growing company. Express was not alone in searching for cheaper ways to cover workers for injuries at a reduced claims cost. A third need identified by the new leadership team was the necessity to consolidate operations in Oklahoma City.[13]

Bob believed that franchising was the key to the future of Express. Long-time employee Tom Gunderson took over control of a franchise sales division that had to maneuver through the legalities of dealing with a system regulated by the Federal Trade Commission (FTC). With the help of attorney Jeri Craig, Express was registered in many states, and its methods of selling franchises were approved by the FTC. Craig had previously helped build the franchising operation of Sonic Industries.[14]

At an Express Services trade show booth are, left to right, national marketing director Richard Roby, Dean Drury, and Colorado franchisee Paul Fangman.

Bob wanted Express to have more integrity than other staffing companies. Because of the unethical behavior he had seen at other staffing operations earlier in his career, he insisted that Express franchise agreements be easy to understand and leave nothing to conjecture. Attorney Craig said, "The agreement that we drafted was unusual because it not only spelled out what we expected from the franchisee, but also provided great detail of what Express would do for the franchisee."[15]

The integrity of the Express franchise agreements was protected because no one received a special deal. Each franchisee was treated the same. Craig said, "Bob and Bill Stoller never tried to hide anything. Everyone within a given franchise registration period was sold the same franchise."[16]

Gunderson created a manual for selling Express franchises. Bob often accompanied Gunderson on visits to potential franchisees. On one trip to San Antonio, Texas, to meet with Chandu Radia, Gunderson rented an economy car and booked rooms at a local Holiday Inn. Gunderson wanted to save the company money. Bob said nothing when Gunderson picked him up in the small car and took him to the hotel. When they completed their business at Radia's office in a downtown high-rise, Radia walked them back to their economy car. After they drove off, Bob told Gunderson, "Never, ever rent an economy car again." Bob was afraid of the impression the economy car left on the potential franchisee.[17]

The Express story is not all about work. There were times of great fun when franchisees and home office personnel gathered for conventions. On one occasion at a convention in Palm Springs, California, Bob was dressed in his nicest suit and made the mistake of joking with people around the pool. Mark Tasler remembered, "The next thing you know, Bob found himself in the pool, with a little help. The first thing he did was grab for his pocket planner because he put his whole life in fine print in that little book."[18]

On a trip to Africa, Bob showed up for a Safari with a starched shirt, a Stetson cowboy hat, and a vest. Tasler said, "The locals did not quite know what to think about him." The trip seemed to go much better when Bob changed into less formal attire for the trip.[19]

Bob was on the road much of the time and had at least one brush with potential tragedy. Once, when he was landing at the DFW Airport in Texas, the pilot of his American Airlines flight informed passengers that he was having trouble lowering the airplane's landing gear. Bob began wondering how well his family could survive without him as the aircraft circled over Dallas with the Boeing 727's crew ripping away carpeting in order to manually release the jammed left main landing gear. Bob's son, Bobby, was only 13 at the time. Bob thought, "How could he make it through his teenage years without a father?"[20]

When the attempts to manually lower the landing gear failed, the crew began putting Bob and the other 80 passengers through emergency landing drills. The passengers removed their shoes to prevent puncture of escape chutes. Fuel was dumped to decrease the potential for explosion and fire. Finally, the crew pulled up the two main landing gears and planned to land somehow on the front nose gear.[21]

"Grab your ankles!" the pilot yelled at the passengers. Then all the lights went out as the pilot and co-pilot successfully landed the airplane. As Bob looked out the window at a stream of fire trucks and emergency vehicles lined up along the runway, he thanked God for the rescue. After the plane rolled to a stop, Bob saw smoke billowing from underneath the airplane. The passengers were quickly removed, with only two injuries.[22]

Bob benefited from the harrowing experience. In exiting the airplane, he lost his alligator skin shoes. When he informed American Airlines of the loss, the company gave him a lifetime platinum card.

Back with his family, Bob focused on Nedra and his children. He promised to plan more quality family time in the midst of expansion of his company. He literally blocked off time on his calendar for family activities.

In 1986, Express moved into a new national headquarters building at 6300 Northwest Expressway in Oklahoma City. "The building is so big," Bob conjectured, "we'll never fill it."

Business boomed and soon the building was full of new Express employees.

The phenomenal growth put great demands on the home office team to service the family of franchisees. The marketing department enhanced its tools under the direction of Richard Roby and Linda Haneborg, who began as assistant director of the communications department in 1988.

Haneborg left a job at an Oklahoma City television station to join Express. She was sold on the advantages of working for Express by Gean Atkinson, the director of communications, who was excited about the potential of Haneborg working for the company.

Haneborg had been trying to sell Bob advertising for two years. During a 90-minute conversation she found him to be a most gracious and accepting person. She could "taste" the huge contract she was about to sell Express. However, at the end of the meeting, Bob told Haneborg, "Why don't you call me back next week and we'll get together on this advertising thing."23

For two years, Haneborg called on Bob but could never get past Carol Lane, "the most incredible gatekeeper on earth." Haneborg never sold Bob any advertising but, in her initial interview for the job at Express, Bob recognized her persistence. She got the job.24

To help franchisees create a consistent brand image, a Yellow Pages program with advertising designs was developed. Three quarterly newsletters, *Expressions, Exchange,* and *Extra,* targeted separate audiences. *Expressions* was a formal house organ, *Exchange* was for clients of franchisees, and *Extra* focused on associates.

Numerous press releases publicizing the company's advances were produced. Haneborg also edited a weekly newsletter, *Inside Track.* Although Express still had less than 100 offices, placing

ABOVE: Left to right, Janet Baxter, Dave Gillogly, and Linda Haneborg at the 1988 National Association of Temporary Services annual convention.

and billing Yellow Page advertisements was a major project. The work was done manually.

At this time, the first national television spot commercial was produced. Haneborg remembered, "It was such an exciting time. Bob encouraged us to build the brand of Express in a way that would set us apart from the competition. We went to Hollywood to produce a product of national significance and acclaim."[25] Thus, the recognizable phrase of "I gotta job!" was born.

In 1989, Gean Atkinston left Express and Haneborg was charged with the responsibility

of starting fresh in the company's approach to external and internal communications. She selected a new advertising agency and hired new designers for corporate materials. Soon, Express was winning the top communications awards from industry organizations.[26]

Haneborg literally changed the face of Express in the eyes of consumers, franchisees, and competitors. Bob said, "She put us on the map from the competitors' standpoint. They saw us winning awards and they began competing for them." Haneborg successfully carried out Bob's philosophy of, "If you put the right face on a company and follow it up with the same amount or more service, then you become a great company."[27]

Left to right, Mark Tasler, Bob Funk, and Chris Corrigan visit alongside the tennis court at an Express convention.

Express made room for young people to grow in the company. When Scott Davis accepted his first position as a sales representative, he felt good about his future. He remembered, "From the moment I met Bob during the initial interview, I knew in the pit of my stomach it would be a tremendous opportunity for a young man like me to be around such a high caliber person." Davis, along with Cindy Fairchild and Sandra VanZant, are vice presidents for Oklahoma at Express.[28]

Harvey Homsey, now Express vice president of franchise systems, began with the company in 1989 and immediately felt a special closeness to Bob. Homsey said, "From the day I interviewed, he took me under his wing and helped guide me. I always knew I could walk in his office for advice."[29]

Homsey was one of the executives who began traveling with Bob. "He always made sure everything was taken care of," Homsey said, "from airplane seats to hotel rooms to cabs and food." During dinners far from home Bob would share from his heart his true feelings about his business, family, and life. He told of his successes and mistakes and how it bothered him that he had spent so much time away from his family while building the company.[30]

Express assumed a major role in national industry organizations. The National Association of Personnel Services (NAPS) was founded in 1961 and is the staffing industry's oldest association. NAPS was created to represent the industry in legislation pending before Congress and state legislatures, to create a structure of ethical practices for industry self-regulation, and to build public and business awareness of the value of personnel services.[31]

Express also became involved in the American Staffing Association (ASA), a group that promoted the interests of temporary staffing agencies through lobbying, public relations,

LEFT: Training Director Art Atkinson, left, and franchisee Linda Sasser of Austin, Texas, ham it up for cameras at a national sales meeting. Sasser is now Express vice president of sales and marketing.

BELOW: Early Express employees Sandra VanZant, left, and Vonda Wolff.

setting ethical standards, and providing education. ASA had been known formerly as the National Association of Temporary Services (NATS and NATSS).[32]

Bob was more determined than ever to build his company and reward his employees. However, an unexpected bump in the road nearly spelled disaster for Bob's dream.

Bill Stoller, left, and Bob
compare notes during
the 1989 annual Express
Services convention.

Twelve

CRITICAL TIMES

SEVERAL UNEXPECTED EVENTS IN THE LATE 1980S nearly doomed Express. The near-tragedy occurred even though the company was growing. The growth came despite the effects of several years of recession in Oklahoma and across the nation. Seemingly, many negatives encountered by other Oklahoma companies turned into positives for Express, especially in the area of hiring top managers. Often Bob was able to hire experienced managers at half the normal salary because of the lack of management jobs in the state.

The young company almost turned its first profit in 1987, but a $350,000 write-off because of a bad receivable at an office in Citrus Heights, California, delayed the dream of becoming profitable.[1] The temporary business was growing exponentially in the nation because cagey business owners and managers learned they could increase cash flow, by paying payroll a month later, and pass off much of the workers' compensation costs to the staffing agency.[2]

One problem that adversely affected Express was the loss of a few high-ranking employees who were disloyal to Bob and tried to inappropriately benefit from his good nature. Even though the overwhelming majority of Bob's managers were unquestionably loyal to him, a few disappointed him.[3]

A training director quit her position at Express and bought a franchise from a competitor. Another executive hid the fact that he had purchased a percentage of a competing business. When Bob discovered the truth, the man was fired on the spot. Other longtime employees took advantage of the contacts they had made at Express and opened their own competing offices.[4]

Bob always had hired top people with loyalty, not skill, as the priority consideration. His belief is, "You can take a loyal person and teach him skills. You can't take a skilled person and teach him loyalty." Bob recognized that new employees usually did not develop loyalty for the first two years. But once they did, it was a two-way street. He said, "If I found they were loyal to the company, then it was up to me to prove that I was loyal to them."[5]

A particularly good, or bad, example of disloyalty is the case of a 20-year veteran regional developer who decided to set up a staffing company on the side and run some of the employment contracts through that entity. The man received 100 percent of the sale, rather than 60 percent if the contract was with Express. "It was absolute greed," Bob said, "He just thought he was a little smarter than the rest of us." When the scheme was discovered, the Express contract was terminated.[6]

In the rare instances of disloyalty, Bob's feelings were hurt, but only temporarily. He never lost his passion for making certain his managers and employees were well taken care of. He instituted a base-salary bonus compensation system. He wanted everyone in an office to have a livable, guaranteed base salary. He also wanted to create a spirit of teamwork by having a bonus system for the entire office. The marketing representatives, the office staff, and the manager all enjoyed a bonus for working as a team and meeting or exceeding production expectations.[7]

By 1988, workers' compensation, recapitalization, and consolidation of operations in Oklahoma City were on the minds of Bob, Bill Stoller, Jim Gray, and chief operating officer Dale Mitchell. Bob planned a retreat to discuss those vital issues that would spell the future of Express.

Bob and Mitchell were not "on the same page" for the direction of the company.[8] Bob believed he needed outside help to remedy the workers' compensation problem that had arisen because insurance rates were rising in a dramatic fashion. He hired Dave Gillogly as a consultant to primarily work on finding a solution to the workers' compensation dilemma. Gillogly had been commissioner of the Oklahoma State Insurance Fund which provided workers' compensation coverage for a large portion of employees in Oklahoma. He also had served on the staff of Oklahoma Governor David Boren and had several years of business experience in the oil and gas industry.

From the beginning, Bob and Gillogly formed a great team. Bob remembered, "He had great people skills, was a good listener, was steady, analyzed problems in an expert fashion, and his value system was the same as mine."[9] Because of his humble personality, Gillogly developed a close working relationship with franchisees. They liked him because he listened to their problems and came up with solutions. Bob said, "Dave had a big heart for franchisees."[10]

Gillogly began his service for Express on his 41st birthday, February 15, 1988. He appeared at the annual Express convention and alerted franchises of the growing workers' compensation problem. Within a few months, Gillogly replaced Mitchell as chief operating officer.

For years, Express had been able to buy a guaranteed cost workers' compensation policy. However, the national workers' compensation picture changed because of a period of high loss, low investment earnings, and a higher cost of reinsurance. Express was not able to buy a guaranteed cost policy for 1989. Instead, its only option was to purchase a "retro" policy in which the up-front premium could be raised if claims exceeded expectations. In effect, it was a modified self-insurance plan.[11]

The potential difficulty for Express was that the company, not the franchisees, was responsible for paying workers' compensation premiums, regardless of the claims experience. The franchisees were free to choose their own customers, including high-risk and hazardous employment that sometimes resulted in large injury claims.[12]

The spiraling costs of workers' compensation coverage became critical. The shrinking workers' compensation market and the rapid growth of Express combined for a near-fatal demise of Express. Gillogly reflected, "The celebration of our rapid growth was quickly followed by the morning after hangover with mounting funding needs."[13]

As higher workers' compensation rates adversely affected the bottom line of Express, Bob and Gillogly began sharing the problem in more detail with franchisees. Express could not absorb the increased premiums. Gillogly remembered, "This led not only to a financial crisis, but a crisis of confidence with the franchisees. They neither understood nor cared about our crisis." Franchisees had grown accustomed to paying a certain price for workers' compensation and believed they could not successfully compete with other staffing agencies if they were asked to pay part of the increased insurance costs.[14]

In the spring of 1989, Gillogly and others used much of their time at the Express annual convention to teach franchisees

Bob believed in strong promotions to motivate his workforce. Trips to exotic destinations were used as a prime motivator.

about client selecting from both the safety and credit perspectives. Gillogly said, "We taught them to say no, to discern and walk away from bad businesses. We asked them to run their businesses, not let their clients run their businesses." Express began enforcing provisions of the Franchise Agreement that allowed the company to reject certain clients on the basis of credit and safety risks.[15]

The most significant event that could have brought the end of Express arose in September, 1989, when CNA Insurance Company (CNA) told Express that $5 million in premiums was owed. Express was given until March 1 of the following year to pay the huge premium. Bob and his management team had no idea where he could raise $5 million.

He had no success with any of his banking connections so he began traveling around the country trying to sell a piece of the company. He never had wanted to surrender control of the company to outside investors, but he was desperate. Bob did not gloss over the situation with his top people—Express had a major problem that, if not solved quickly, would force the company into bankruptcy.[16]

Gillogly discovered that eight Express offices were responsible for nearly half the work-related injuries that were driving up premiums for the group policy. One of the first things he did was to treat each office on an individual basis for determining workers' compensation premiums. For example, an office that had very few claims paid a small premium. Conversely, an office that provided workers for hazardous employment and incurred heavy losses paid a much higher premium.

Gillogly gathered the loudest complainers and made them a committee to solve the workers' compensation problem. Express began collecting the individual modified premiums before the end of 1989. Almost immediately, the higher premiums for high-risk offices began to raise money to retire the $5 million debt.[17]

CNA extended the deadline for payment to June 1, 1990. With the increased premiums and an assessment on each office, the $5 million was paid. Bob remembered, "There were times when we doubted we could pay the bill. The company was in jeopardy. If CNA had pressed us, we would have been out of business!"[18]

The increased workers' compensation premiums made local offices examine the type of workers they were providing for employers. In many cases, franchisees made conscious decisions to change their book of business. No longer were local offices interested in providing workers in extremely hazardous positions that resulted in huge workers' compensation insurance premiums.[19]

Sales continued to skyrocket. Express became a prime example of the free enterprise system. Express was growing at a much faster pace than its competitors because of outside one-on-one relationship marketing. Competitors were not willing to spend money for outside marketing representatives. Bob said, "We were ahead of the game because we hired outside people. Our competitor might be knocking on 15 or 20 doors a week—we were knocking on 100. The more doors you knock on, the more businesses you sell. It's a matter of numbers."[20]

The phenomenal growth did cause concern for Jim Gray who believed Express was expanding too quickly. He told Bob, "With the sudden growth, we can't keep up with the bookkeeping and accounting procedures. The banks won't give us any more money to finance the growth."[21]

Bob did not want to do anything to hinder Express' growth. His usual reply to Gray was, "It doesn't matter. We'll find a bank. We'll get done what needs to be done!" Bob appreciated his people working up to 80 hours a week. He remembered, "I certainly didn't want to slow down our people's passion!" Because of the difference of opinion in how fast to grow the company, Bob and Stoller purchased Gray's interest in Express.[22]

With operations consolidated in Oklahoma City, Tom Richards became an important cog in keeping Express alive. No one from the former accounting center in Colorado moved to Oklahoma City, so Richards, a certified public accountant and former chief financial officer of First City Bank in Oklahoma City, had to build an accounting and information technology center from scratch. Richards personally carried the first computer into the new accounting center.[23]

Bob credits Richards with making possible the delivery of payroll and accounting services to the growing list of franchisees. Bob said, "Tom has more knowledge, from the financial prospective, than anyone in the industry worldwide."[24]

The workers' compensation issue had compounded the financial crisis for Express. Fast growth meant a growing need for cash. The faster the company grew, the wider became the gap between expenditure and income. A temporary worker had to be paid each week, but companies paid their bill once a month. Eventually, Express outgrew their method of obtaining funding from local banks that became nervous as Express needed more and more money to keep its doors open. The company scrambled for alternate sources of income to meet a weekly payroll of millions of dollars.

During one particular week of crisis, more than $1 million was needed to make payroll. Bob had mortgaged everything he owned and had run out of options. Gillogly offered to put $250,000, everything he had, into the company. Bob refused, but Stoller came up with the money to keep the lender from "pulling the plug." Stoller remembered, "We all pitched in to do what needed to be done. Here was a way I could be instrumental in assuring the future security of the company."[25]

Scrambling to make payroll caused Bob and his top managers many sleepless nights. If they ever missed payroll, they would have been out of business. Even the failure to meet one week's payroll would have violated their Franchise Agreement, destroyed the system, and invited huge litigation liabilities.

Each month, as franchisees paid their share of increased workers' compensation premiums, and as sales increased, the funding crisis lessened. By the end of 1991, Express was adequately capitalized so there was no weekly worry about making payroll.[26]

Express Executive Vice President of Sales Bob Fellinger and Tom Richards, Executive Vice President of Operations and CFO, discuss the exponential growth of Express Services, Inc.

Left to right, Lars Nurman and Midrael Haglind, of Sweden's largest temporary help firm Teamwork, sign a 1992 agreement with Express Personnel to operate a staffing business in that country. Bob, right, looks on. *Courtesy Oklahoma Publishing Company.*

Thirteen

A JOB FOR EVERY PERSON AND A PERSON FOR EVERY JOB

IN 1993, BOB LOOKED BACK ON THE FIRST DECADE of Express Personnel Services and was pleased with the progress of the company. Express had more than 200 franchise offices with annual sales of more than $325 million. The Express companies included Express Personnel Services and Express Professional Staffing. In its first decade, Express already was the nation's eighth-largest company in the temporary staffing industry.

Express offered a full range of staffing services, including temporary placement, evaluation hire, flexible staffing, and searches for executives. Also part of the group of companies under the Express banner was Express Travel Service, a travel agency in Oklahoma City.[1]

As the economy recovered from another recession in the early 1990s, Express began adding franchises at a record pace. Bob and his management team recognized that quick and comprehensive training of franchisees and their employees was the key to their success. In 1992, Art Atkinson became vice president of a newly-restructured training and development department. The following year, MaryAnn Spencer Manning became director of training.[2]

BELOW: *Expressions* was one of several publications of Express Services to keep its employees and franchisees well informed on new marketing directions.

Vol. IX, NO. 4 • 1991

OFFICE RANKINGS INSIDE

EXPRESSIONS
E T C • E T C • E T C

Attendance at 98% Indicates High Interest in...
1991 REGIONAL MEETINGS

CHICAGO

Your Energy...Focus on Business!" meeting was a great success, thanks to the enthusiastic involvement of speakers, breakout leaders and roundtable presenters.

"*Channel Your Energies,*" theme for the 1991 Regional Meetings, used a TV program theme with the "Gong Show" being one of the hilarious moments on the agenda.

In **Atlanta**, brand new owners blended with veterans from the Southern offices to explore new ideas in marketing with promotions, sharing those that had proved most effective. Small in number (15 in attendance) but powerful (with new all-time highs) in a group, they enjoyed a great regional meeting.

⬤he eye-opener on Saturday morning was hearing Kelly Heflin relate the dream she'd had the night before. In her dream, everyone was held captive in the hotel and Kelly talked their way out. And, the

The real stars of the meeting were Lynne Scofield and a disguised industrial worker (a.k.a. Jerry Scofield) presenting their Workers' Compensation Loss Control Program. Lynne was in grand form, as she always is, eagerly presenting well-researched information that could have a dramatic impact on every office's bottom line.

The Colorado, Wyoming, Missouri, Montana and Texas folks attending the **Denver** Regional "Channeled Their Energies" into high gear Friday

PORTLAND

DENVER

experience at Aunt Pitty-Pat's Porch was not soon to be forgotten, especially "Gwen," the waitress who demonstrated "true customer service."

Over 100 eager Express Services' professionals attended the Regional Meeting in **Dallas**, Texas. Held at the Marriott Quorum, the "Channel

when they had a refreshing visit from the resident fitness guru. Everyone enthusiastically joined in the exercise sequence, all the while noticing what remarkable shape their "Lumbar Leader" was in.

Continued

At the 1992 Express convention, the theme was "Race to Success." To make a point, Bob stripped down to racing shorts and jogging shoes to underscore the importance of racing to success.

Atkinson said, "Our goal in training was to get new franchisees out of the gates and running in the first 90 days." To achieve that goal, Atkinson had to call upon representatives from every department at national headquarters for their expertise. A franchisee with no prior working knowledge of the staffing industry had to leave the training period with

RIGHT: Bob, in cowboy hat and bandana, welcomes franchisee Bernie Harrington of Aberdeen, South Dakota to an Express convention.

substantial information about recruiting, selling, and service. As a hallmark of the training, ethical behavior was emphasized for new franchisees.[3]

Each training class, at what later became known as Express University, becomes a tightly knit group. During training, the franchisees are housed in the same facility, travel to and from training sessions together, and eat at least two meals a day together.[4]

After graduating from high school in Piedmont, Julie Funk attended college at the University of Central Oklahoma. In 1999, she married Christopher "Chris" Bridges. Today, Julie is a mother of two beautiful children, Bailey and Bowen, and works at Arden.

Bobby Funk graduated from high school in Piedmont and attended Oklahoma Baptist University. Today, he resides in Reno, Nevada, where he is a marketing representative for the Reno Express office, working with Dan Gunderson, son of Tom Gunderson. Bobby said "Dad taught me many life lessons, but the greatest is that I should treat every person I meet with respect and that my major concern be about helping other people."

Express expanded internationally in 1992 and was perceived in the industry as a much larger and more progressive company than before. The first venture into the international arena was in Sweden where, with the help of the Express system, Teamwork became the nation's largest personnel system and grew from $9 million to $43 million in annual sales in just three years.[5]

That same year, Express expanded into Russia, providing franchise help to find management-level employees who could work with American companies in a Russian world. At the time, temporary help was outlawed in Russia. Mark Tasler, who helped train Russian franchisees, said, "Russia was a good experience for Express, a marketing boost for us. We taught them how to run a business using our standards."[6]

In the end, the Swedish and Russian experiences were disappointing to Bob and Express. After Express had turned around the Swedish company from near failure to a huge annual sales volume, the company sold to an Express competitor for $42 million. Even though Express received $2 million of the sales price, Bob was disappointed. He said, "It was the loyalty issue that cost us."[7]

The Russian situation was similar. Bob and others personally spent a great deal of time restructuring the Russian business and teaching the Russians that capitalism worked and that a Christian value-based company was good for everyone involved. After the Russian company was operating 14 offices, it decided to stop paying royalties to Express. Unfortunately, because of the inept state of the Russian justice system, Express had no reasonable chance to successfully sue for the royalties. Express just walked away.[8]

By positioning Express as a full-service human resource solution, the company continued to grow, despite minor setbacks from dealing with the Swedes and Russians. Bob's goal was to

Bob, center, watches Elena Novikova sign a partnership agreement between Express Personnel and her Russian personnel agency, ANCOR, in November, 1992. At left is ANCOR manager Vladimir Gelten. *Courtesy Oklahoma Publishing Company.*

provide a complete package including staffing, training, workers' compensation advice, and virtual human resources and payroll services.[9]

Even though sales and service lines were expanding, Bob found it important to take time to instill in each new employee or franchisee the Express philosophy of providing quality, ethical service. Bob made it a priority to interview all new employees at the corporate headquarters and at each of his personally-owned

RIGHT: Left to right, Southern Nazarene University President Loren Gresham, Linda Gresham, Nedra Funk, and Bob Funk, at a 1993 Oklahoma City social event.

BELOW: Bob spent much of his business day on the telephone, encouraging franchisees who needed a pep talk. *Courtesy Oklahoma Publishing Company.*

BELOW: The Express Services vice presidents in 1993. Left to right, front row, Tom Gunderson, Tom Richards, Dave Kuker, and Art Atkinson. Back row, Linda Haneborg, Carol Lane, Jerry Baird, and David Baird.

32 offices in Oklahoma, Texas, and Arkansas. His philosophy was not to grow by merger and acquisitions. Instead, he focused on growing the company organically to maintain its strong corporate culture. Today, Bob's personal touch continues. No matter how hectic his schedule is, he still interviews all applicants.[10]

Bob personally met with many potential franchisees from around the country. Sometimes the meetings were "normal"

An Express newsletter announced the company's first sweepstakes program in 1993.

business encounters. On other occasions, the franchisee never forgot the moment of meeting Bob. Jim Britton was only 28 years old when Bob picked him up at the airport in Oklahoma City. Britton remembered, "This tall lanky guy had the biggest grin ever. We got into his Cadillac Eldorado, the biggest car I'd ever seen, and buzzed through town with a lot of energy. We visited three offices and raced everywhere we went."[11]

Britton's exciting ride through central Oklahoma was overshadowed by the relationship he observed between Bob and his employees. Britton said, "It was obvious that Bob was gracious, willing to share, and completely open with his people. There was a bond there that I could not explain nor had I read about in the best salesmanship books of the era."[12]

Other interviews with potential franchisees were interesting. Sisters Bonne McArthur and Elizabeth Shinn met with Bob in his Oklahoma City office and were taken back by all the cowboy statues in the office. Bonne said, "Not knowing Bob was a Republican, we of course had to blurt out how much we loved the President Kennedy Camelot era. It is amazing he ever gave us the nod to purchase the franchise in our home city of Everett, Washington. However, we soon learned Bob was looking at our business ability, not our political affiliation."[13]

As Express expanded rapidly, the decision of Bob and Bill Stoller to stay fully franchised again proved to be a secret of the company's success. When Express was formed from the ashes of Acme Personnel, Bob observed that franchisees were more aggressive in their marketing than their corporate counterparts. The emphasis on franchising also made sense in that local franchisees knew their cities and towns better than home office managers and could build relationships better and quicker. Bob also realized early on that the only way to grow a business and to help others was by being partners in profitability with them.[14]

Ultimate optimism was an arrow in Bob's quiver of successfully building Express. Jim Britton said, "He blew me away when he walked up to me and said, 'Jim, you're doing great, but I can double your business in six months.' He was right. Bob never sees the downside of anything—he always sees the possibility."[15]

Express was an innovator in the human resources business. All client billing and payroll is completed at the corporate headquarters—unique in the franchising world. Every employee at Express knows that he or she is expected to keep the company's commitments to franchisees. Franchisees become a community ambassador for Express. Bob said, "Their business success is a testimony to the companies and individuals they interact with on a daily basis."[16]

International recognition has allowed Express to be featured in numerous publications. Positioning himself and Express as honest, ethical, and hard working has enabled Bob to highlight the positive aspects of franchising. That allows Bob to operate the business on the basis of "doing the right thing" whether or not it results in the highest economic benefit. Under the Express model, franchisees can run their businesses according to their values beyond principles of profitability most normal businesses enforce. "We've proven," Bob said, "that we can value people more than the bottom line and have seen the payoff."[17]

Bob, blindfolded, draws the winner of the company's first sweepstakes. The drawing was staged on the front lawn of the Express Personnel Services office on Northwest Highway in Oklahoma City.

The Express management team accompanied Bob to Canada for a joyous celebration as the company expanded to that country. Left to right, Linda Haneborg, Dave Gillogly, Bob, Bill Stoller, and Tom Gunderson.

Fourteen

STRENGTH FOR THE FUTURE

BOB HAS SHARED HIS PASSION FOR HELPING PEOPLE with his franchisees. Time and again stories have been told of how employees and managers of local franchise operations have carried out the Bob Funk tradition of assisting those in need.

In Jeremy Thacker's Express office in Jonesboro, Arkansas, one of the staffing consultants had been taking a temporary worker to her job each day because her old car was in need of repair. When asked about Christmas, the worker said there was no money for Christmas presents for her five daughters—there would be no Christmas tree. The children, understanding their mother's plight, only wished for a puppy. The mother was heartbroken.[1]

When the consultant returned to the office, she shared the sad story with the rest of the staff. Things began rolling. The office staff gave the family a Christmas tree, and the local humane society arranged for the children to adopt a puppy. Coats, gloves, and toys were purchased for the children. Express employees bought dog food for the puppy. Even the company where Express had placed the temporary worker got into the action. Company personnel took her to a local Wal-Mart and bought more Christmas gifts. A car was donated to the woman. When it was discovered the car needed tires, the local Firestone dealer donated them. Overwhelmed by the generosity of so many people, Thacker said, "If nothing else good happens this year, it makes this job worth every minute to know we were able to show kindness to someone in need."[2]

Randall and Pat Camp own the Express franchise in Ocala, Florida, and have put into practice Bob's principles of using a God-given opportunity to help their community. When their front office coordinator, a single mom, needed transportation, they bought a car for her. Each year, the Camps contribute money to their Express Care Fund to help needy people who come through their doors. Local office employees determine how the money is distributed. The fund helps workers buy clothing, gasoline, and food.[3]

The Camps' offices also collect clothing for temporary workers who might have the right skills for a job, but not the right wardrobe. The Camps' faith is shared with team members and prospective workers. A corporate chaplain is available for weekly visits with staff members and counsels workers when appropriate.[4]

A staffing consultant in Oklahoma interviewed an applicant who needed a job closer to home because he could not afford the expense of a long commute. There was a job perfect for the applicant, but it required a high school diploma. The consultant informed the applicant he could take the GED test the following day, but the man did not have money for the test. The consultant went to her purse and gave the applicant the money for the test so he could improve his life. She did not expect repayment. However, two weeks later, the man returned with his GED and repaid the consultant. He then obtained a higher paying job closer to home.[5]

The Express franchise in Helena, Montana, formerly owned by Doug and Kathy Kelley, made a difference in the lives of many. The Kelleys and office manager, Lynne Johnson, began a unique program to find employment for men and women who came from the Los Angeles Training Center in California, a living center for people recovering from addiction.[6]

Because the workers wishing a fresh start had no credit history, the Helena office purchased a large home and a seven-unit apartment building to house them. At first, the Express office even paid utilities for the workers who were getting adjusted to living a normal lifestyle. Johnson, who was called "Mama Rambo" by the relocated employees, said, "There have been some disappointments, with workers failing their commitment, but those disappointments have been offset by knowing that many people have risen to the challenge of a fresh start."[7]

In 1997, with offices setting records on a weekly basis, Bob and his vice presidents announced $1 billion as a reasonable annual sales target. The 300th Express office opened in Ottawa, Canada, one of several expansions into America's neighbor to the north.

The Canadian expansion has been greatly aided by Christine Menard, already a veteran in the staffing business when she joined forces with Express. Menard was not certain she needed to affiliate with Bob and Express in Canada. Then she heard him speak. She remembered, "He was so open and honest. His charisma drew me into the Express family. I knew from the first moment that I could trust this man. His handshake was as good as a written contract."[8]

Menard quickly discovered Bob's secret to attracting good franchisees. She said, "Bob has a way of seeing into your real heart of what you really believe in. He has the ability of recognizing a good person when he sees them—both in their beliefs and their capability of being a good business person."[9]

The concept of separate training classes for field operations and sales staff was unveiled and regional training centers were established. It was a challenge for corporate headquarters staff to keep up with rapid expansion. When Cyndi Framme became National Sales Manager, five franchise offices were opened during her first month, before she had completed her own training.

Recognizing the need for a strategic plan to guide growth that was "bursting at the seams," Express created a Strategic Sales department, later renamed Business Development. Framme became vice president for business development and implemented plans to solidify and expand the Express client base, including working with Fortune 1000 companies through multiple office locations. To strengthen the Express business development focus at the franchise level, franchisees were encouraged to focus on a top 10 client list.[10]

President and chief operating officer Dave Gillogly retired in 1999, closing out 10 years of service to the company. Under his watchful eye, Express had reached $1 billion in annual revenues and successfully rolled out the Q3 automated computer system that literally revolutionized the business by making it quicker and easier to generate payroll. In his closing memo to employees, Gillogly wrote, "Love people and help them to succeed."[11]

Successfully moving into the advanced computer age with the Q3 system, which took 10 years and $11 million to develop, again reminded Bob how much his co-workers meant to the growth and success of Express. When the new version of Q3 was unveiled in September, 1999, the normal bugs in the system created huge customer service problems. Terri Weldon was manager of customer service and guided a skilled team of in-house computer and customer service representatives in smoothing out

In 2002, Express moved into a new headquarters building on the Northwest Expressway in Oklahoma City.

problems. Many of the people slept at Express headquarters during critical periods of getting the new computer system online.

In 2002, Express employees moved 18 years of files, photos, and assorted papers into a new 60,000-square-foot headquarters building placed majestically behind a small lake on the Northwest Expressway in Oklahoma City. As the company grew, employees had been scattered in three different locations in northwest Oklahoma City. With the new location, all headquarters personnel were housed under one roof. Adjacent to the corporate headquarters was the Express Events Center, a state-of-the-art meeting center.

Express celebrated its 20th anniversary in 2003 with an extended national convention in Oklahoma City. Television minister Dr. Robert Schuller was the guest speaker at the annual Prayer Breakfast. Baseball star Cal Ripkin, Jr., and motivator Amanda Gore were among the general session speakers at the convention.[12]

In 2003, Express Personnel saw global sales top $1 billion for the second time. The following year, sales were up again, to $1.3 billion.

However, not each moment of 2004 was rosy for Bob, especially when he feared he was having a heart attack on a trip to the South Pacific. He barely made his connection in Los Angeles and his left arm was numb by the time his plane landed in Fiji. Bob stayed the entire eight days on the trip to recognize employees for their production. Doctors in Fiji could not find anything wrong with his EKG, but Bob continued to suffer and worry.[13]

When Bob returned to Oklahoma City, doctors ran another EKG, which also showed no signs of a heart attack. He was urged to undergo a treadmill stress test but Bob put it off for a couple of days to take care of business. When the stress test was completed, doctors found two of Bob's arteries were almost completely blocked, a condition that was relieved by inserting stents. Bob took two days off and was back on the job the following Monday.[14]

In October, 2005, Express awarded its 500th franchise, joining an elite circle of American franchisors with more than 500 units. Express was in three foreign countries, Canada, South Africa, and Australia, and employed 300,000 people annually.

The growth of the Express franchise operation can be traced to the company's leadership. There is a special relationship between Bob and Express franchise holders. Attorney Sam Hammons, who handles governmental relations for Express, observed, "Many people call him 'Uncle Bob.' He is always affable and displays an easy approachability amidst the crowds of people surrounding him at International Leadership Conferences and other events."[15]

One of the reasons franchisees appreciate Bob is his willingness to address the myriad of political and regulatory issues confronting Express and its franchise owners. Bob has recognized the need to invest his time to visit local, state, and national political leaders about issues of concern. Hammons said, "It would be difficult to find any business leader in the entire country who has done more to educate political leaders about the staffing industry."[16]

However, Bob's involvement in government runs deeper than just protecting the interest of franchise owners and thousands of Express employees. He is deeply concerned about the moral, social, political, and cultural life of the United States. Hammons said, "He understands instinctively the link between a healthy culture and good government and is willing to spend his valuable time for the betterment of both."[17]

Former Oklahoma Governor Frank Keating, in an Express Personnel corporate history written by Lu Hollander, said of Express' phenomenal success, "The Express story is about people seeking a better tomorrow, a more secure future, and a proud place before their friends and families as wage earners and solid providers...Express represents the new America. It looks beyond race and creed and sex and nationality and says, 'If you want to work, we have a place for you.'"[18]

Oklahoma Congresswoman Mary Fallin said, "Bob is the consummate, passionate entrepreneur. He puts the golden touch on any new idea!"[19]

Why did Express succeed, when other companies failed? "It was Bob's vision and heart that made it happen," said Bob Fellinger, Express executive vice president of sales. Fellinger, a former banker, came on board in 1994 as an Express franchisee after retiring. Bob subscribes to Fellinger's three-way test of every function of headquarters—Does it help franchisees increase their sales? Does it help bring profitability to franchisees? And does it help Express award new franchises?[20]

Bob sees nothing but "straight up" for the future of the worldwide staffing business, especially in Europe where businesses are hesitant about hiring permanent workers because of short work weeks, eight-week vacations, and huge benefit packages. In countries such as France, temporary workers are becoming the norm.[21]

Fellinger agrees with Bob's assessment of the future. "We have an incredible model," he said. "Since we are privately owned, we can look at the big picture with a long-term view. We are not driven by Wall Street. Everything about Express is based upon relationships."[22]

In 2007, Express is the fifth-largest staffing agency in the United States. Bob's goal—he wants achieved by 2009—is for Express to be the top company of its kind in the nation with annual sales of $4 billion.

He sees real growth potential in Express providing not just workers, but complete human resource management services. Express Business Solutions, a new division, was created as a separate entity to teach companies how to properly hire workers and how to handle such issues as employment discrimination, wrongful termination, and workers' compensation. Bob says, "Most entrepreneurs did not become successful because they want to manage people. They became entrepreneurs because they had a great idea." The Express Business Solutions goal is to provide human resource solutions to entrepreneurs whose ideas have brought them success.

Looking back at his first 23 years of what has become one of the world's leading staffing companies, Bob said:

In the staffing arena, I think we've given integrity to the industry. No longer are we considered "flesh peddlers." I also think we have shown that we can develop and grow rapidly and keep our culture which is not an easy thing to do. We've been able to withstand phenomenal growth and maintain our Christian values. And, I have been able to fulfill my dream of helping people succeed.[23]

Bob Funk has come full circle. He began his adult life wanting to be a minister—and has spent his life ministering to and providing jobs for millions of people.

Express employees always have been encouraged to give back to their community. Bob, right, announced a corporate gift of $50,000 for a new scholarship program for Russian students at Seattle Pacific University, Bob's alma mater.

ABOVE: In 1995, Express inaugurated its highest company award, named for Bob's first boss at Acme Personnel, Gordon Blair. Left to right, Bill Stoller, Gordon Blair, Jeanne Blair, Nedra Funk, and Bob Funk.

RIGHT: A special birthday celebration for Bob in 2003. Left to right, Carol Lane, Cindy Fairchild, and Linda Haneborg.

RIGHT: Matthew Penfold prepares to sign franchise documents for Express Personnel franchises in Australia. Seated right is Bob Funk. Standing, left to right, Bill Stoller, Fred Muse, and Doug Eaton.

Bob, appearing as the Biblical character, Moses, in his keynote presentation for the 1998 Express International Leadership Conference.

Bob, his hat, and his Clydesdale—
a perfect combination at his New Mexico
ranch. *Courtesy Dr. John Edwards.*

Fifteen

BOB—THE COWBOY

FROM HIS TEENAGE YEARS, farming had been one of Bob's three goals in life. When he moved to Piedmont, he immediately began looking for pasture land. He never intended to enter the dairy business of which he was so accustomed in Washington, but nevertheless wanted to build a strong herd of cattle on his land in Oklahoma.

Bob settled on Limousin as his breed of cattle. These golden-red cattle are native to the south central part of France in the regions of Limousin and Marche. Because of the rugged and rolling land and harsh climate in that part of France, Limousin cattle evolved into a breed of unusual sturdiness, health, and adaptability. The breed is thousands of years old but American cattlemen only began importing Limousin in the 1960s.[1]

Bob mixed his Limousin with Angus cattle, a breed well known for producing quality beef. Soon after Express Services, Inc. came of age and began prospering, Bob formed Express Ranches to manage as many as 15,000 head of Limousin and Angus cattle and maintain 160,000 acres of grazing land.[2]

The goal of the management of Express Ranches—president Jarold Callahan and his employees—is to improve its herd with constant genetic advances. Each year, Express Ranches tries to design cattle that can bend the curve on calving ease and outstanding body and maternal characteristics. The ranching operation grosses more than $13 million annually in sales of cattle and breeding fees.

In 2006, Express Ranches set a single-day record for heifer sales. One bull brought $263,000, an Oklahoma record. Express Ranches has become the second-largest seed stock producer in the United States and the largest registered Angus producer.[3]

In 1994, when Bob was expanding his ranch near Yukon, he bought a piece of land from H.I. Grimes that contained an old barn built in 1935. The shingles were flapping and roof tiles were falling. The barn was bending over and slumping. The weather vanes were clinging to the building at angles. Bob liked the appearance of the hip-style roof and architecturally

RIGHT: The sign at the entrance of Express Ranches near Yukon, Oklahoma.

BELOW: Bob chose Limousin cattle to anchor his ranching operation. The Limousin breed is thousands of years old.

graceful wings of the barn. A pulley and grapple hook hanging from a window gave the barn charm that made Bob think of saving the structure.[4]

An engineering company quoted Bob a prohibitive amount to restore the barn, but a cattle customer suggested the name of an Amish barn builder in Indiana. Bob contacted David Bontrager and invited him to take a look at the barn. When Bontrager first saw the barn, he told Bob that it would be very expensive to restore it so Bob should consider tearing it down—it would cost more to rehabilitate the barn than to build a new one.[5]

Bob heard stories of the barn from people who lived in the area and was determined to restore it to its original condition. During World War II, horses were trained in the barn for the United States Army. Older neighbors told of the barn being the community gathering spot for dances. When neighbors said, "Please don't tear down the barn—there are too many memories," Bob listened.

Bontrager and several of his 13 children, and their wives, came to Oklahoma to rebuild the large barn. It was a challenge

for the crew from Indiana. Past Oklahoma windstorms had pushed the structure until it was leaning northward by more than four feet. The wind problem was new to the Amish—but rebuilding old barns was not. Using winches and pulleys, the barn was straightened, old windows were replaced, shingles were nailed down or replaced, and the barn had new life. When it was completed, the barn was a landmark for the area and for Express Ranches. Today, the barn contains a gift shop and serves as a welcome center for the Express Clydesdales.[6]

In 1996, on a trip to Canada, Bob fell in love with Clydesdale horses. He bought eight rare black and white Clydesdales and brought them to his Yukon ranch. Within a few years, Bob accumulated more than 50 of the gentle giant horses. To protect

Sale day is a busy day at Express Ranches. This aerial view shows the large barns and expansive parking areas.

Bob with two of his prize Clydesdales. Bob, a tall man himself, is dwarfed by the size of the majestic animals. *Courtesy Dr. John Edwards.*

ABOVE: Bob, one of his Clydesdales, and two youngsters, Emma McDonald and Neil Ash, who were helped by medical personnel at hospitals in the Children's Miracle Network. The Express Personnel Clydesdales help raise money for CMN projects. *Courtesy Dr. John Edwards.*

Bob—The Cowboy   189

them from harsh Oklahoma winters, Bob housed the horses in the Amish-restored barn.[7]

ABOVE: Express Ranches employees care for Bob's Clydesdales in a modern and beautifully-decorated facility. *Courtesy Dr. John Edwards.*

As the Clydesdale herd grew, Bob began receiving requests for

RIGHT: The Funk family at a cattle sale, left to right, Bob, Bobby, Julie, and Nedra.

them to appear at community events, parades, fairs, and equine competitions. Their popularity grew and the stately animals were in constant demand across the country. Bob decided that the Children's Miracle Network (CMN) should benefit from his Clydesdales appearing publicly. At any event where the horses appear, their handlers raise money for CMN.[8]

Since 1999, the Clydesdales have been competing nationally and in Canada, bringing home world-class awards and international recognition. For example, the teams were national six-horse and eight-horse champions at the National Clydesdales Show in Milwaukee, Wisconsin, in 2001. That year, the American Staffing Association, a staffing industry group, awarded the Express Clydesdales its National Public Service Award.[9]

Keeping the Clydesdales in proper health is no small task. Each of the animals' horseshoes are computer cut so each shoe is exact. The shoes weigh about three pounds each and average nine inches wide by more than

eight inches long. The horses, which normally weigh approximately one ton each, are shoed with a leader pad for added support and protection. Each Clydesdale is re-shoed every six weeks.

The Clydesdales pull a hotel coach which is a replica of a coach used by the Crawford House Hotel in Concord, New Hampshire, to carry first-class passengers in 1880. The coach can carry 24 passengers and has two drivers. The horses also pull a replica of an early twentieth century delivery wagon based on a Studebaker design.[10]

Oklahoma City Blazers hockey coach, Doug Sauter, is vice president of Express Clydesdales. With manager, Josh Minshull, and Express corporate event marketing specialist, Debbie Zettlemoyer, the horse operation serves as ambassadors for Express Personnel Services, traveling more than 100,000 miles and making more than 75 appearances each year.[11]

Visitors to the Express Ranch find it impressive. One reporter wrote:

> Head west from Oklahoma City on old 66 to Yukon, and take a trip back through time. Pick your era—the Mother Road, cattle drives of the old West, or maybe even knights in shining armor. After driving through downtown Yukon, go north on Garth Brooks Boulevard...After crossing the North Canadian River, you enter a jaw-dropping landscape. Everything about Express Ranch is BIG—the land, 3,500 acres, the white fences that run on and on, the cattle roaming inside the fences, to the right on a rise, the owner Bob Funk's house, which looks more like a resort hotel, and, of course, the horses. The Clydesdale barn is straight ahead at the intersection of Garth Brooks and Wilshire. When you get out, chances are you'll be greeted by one to three dogs—darned if they aren't big too, but friendly, as is the staff.[12]

By 2006, Bob's ranches had grown to 30,000 acres in four states. The ranching operation was world-renowned for its artificial insemination operation. Bob became president of the board of directors of the North American Limousin Foundation and received the Lifetime Achievement Award from the Oklahoma Limousin Breeders Association in 2001. In 2005, Oklahoma State University's Department of Animal Sciences gave Bob the Distinguished Service Award for his work in becoming an international exporter of genetics and assisting research in the field.

The ranch itself stretches over the central Oklahoma hills and valleys in a magnificent manner. Cutting through the ranch is the remnants of the Chisholm Trail that carried six million cattle north from Texas to the railhead in Abilene, Kansas, from 1867 to 1889. The crown jewel of the ranch is the Funks' 26,000-square-foot home.

For his work in preserving the American West and the heritage of the cowboy, Bob was named vice chairman of the board of the National Cowboy and Western Heritage Museum in Oklahoma City. He also served as a director of the Prix de West Society and was chairman of the museum's awards committee.[13]

Bob established the Express Ranches Progressive Junior Scholarship Program in 1995. Junior exhibitors who purchase show heifers and steers from Express Ranches are eligible for scholarship awards up to $25,000. More than $1.8 million has been awarded to more than 250 youth since the program's inception.[14]

Bob has worked with other youth and livestock supporters such as the Samuel Roberts Noble Foundation and Chesapeake Energy to revitalize the century-old Oklahoma Youth Expo, the largest junior livestock show in America and Oklahoma's largest youth event. The Expo provides scholarship support to hundreds of rural Oklahoma youngsters each year who travel to Oklahoma City during the third week of March to exhibit their livestock at the State Fairgrounds. Bob has realized his goal to provide more than $1.7 million annually in scholarships and awards to participants in the Oklahoma Youth Expo.

Before his untimely death in an airplane accident in 2006, Justin Whitefield, executive director of Oklahoma Youth Expo, said, "Bob never stops dreaming. He now wants to move toward $2 million in annual awards. He saw other states making an impact in the lives of their rural youth and wanted Oklahoma to lead the nation in assisting 4-H and FFA students."[15]

Bob welcomes students who have focused on farming and ranching to visit his ranch and talk about the future of agriculture. He annually participates in programs of the Oklahoma State University College of Agricultural Sciences and Natural Resources in planning information programs for students that include visits to the Express Ranches. Bob likes the idea of being able to show students real-world agriculture.[16]

Another of Bob's longtime ranching friends is retired actor Dale Robertson, an Oklahoma-born movie star who appeared in 63 movies and in more than 400 hours of television shows. Robertson appeared in the *Tales of Wells Fargo, J.J. Starbuck,* and was in the original cast of *Dynasty.*[17]

Robertson, who also owned a horse ranch near Yukon, drove by Bob's ranch one day and introduced himself. Robertson said, "I knew I had met a great man. You just have to go to one of his sales. When he gets up to the microphone at the dinner and entertainment night and you listen to him speak, you know you are you listening to a genuine, friendly man who always thanks his guests, business associates, and friends for helping in his success."[18]

In 2005, Bob was awarded the Honorary American FFA Degree, the highest award of the organization. Bob supported many programs to help student farmers develop an interest in American agriculture. He considered his help of high school and college-age future farmers as repayment for the mentoring he received as a high school FFA student in his hometown of Duvall, Washington.[19]

As part of his ranching heritage, Bob is an early riser. For years he ate many of his early morning breakfasts and business lunches at the Village Inn Pancake House in Oklahoma City. He had his "usual" every morning—oatmeal and white toast or two eggs over well, toast, milk, and coffee. Barbara Smith became his favorite waitress and waited on Bob and his friends and business associates for 20 years.[20]

Barbara and Bob became good friends. Bob often added to Barbara's frog collection, picking up different versions of the amphibian from gift shops around the world. For many years they exchanged Christmas gifts. Barbara said, "For a man who had everything, it was difficult to find him something for Christmas that he didn't have." However, Barbara always found some knickknack for Bob's office.[21]

In 1999, Barbara was having what she described as a "rough" year with health and personal problems. To help the family out of a crisis, Bob gave Barbara a car for Christmas that year. She said, "From that moment, he became an angel for my family and me. My life would not be the same without him."[22]

There is no question that Bob has a big heart and never forgets people who helped him on his way to the top. At another Christmas season, he delivered a fully-loaded recreational vehicle to a very surprised Paul Springfield, the banker who helped him secure a loan to start Express Personnel.

The gift of the vehicle to Springfield is but one of many examples of Bob never forgetting to show his appreciation for friends and associates. Former Oklahoma Governor George Nigh, the first person appointed to the Express Advisory Council, said, "Bob always puts others ahead of himself. When you least expect it, he comes up with a caring and thoughtful reminder of your friendship."[23]

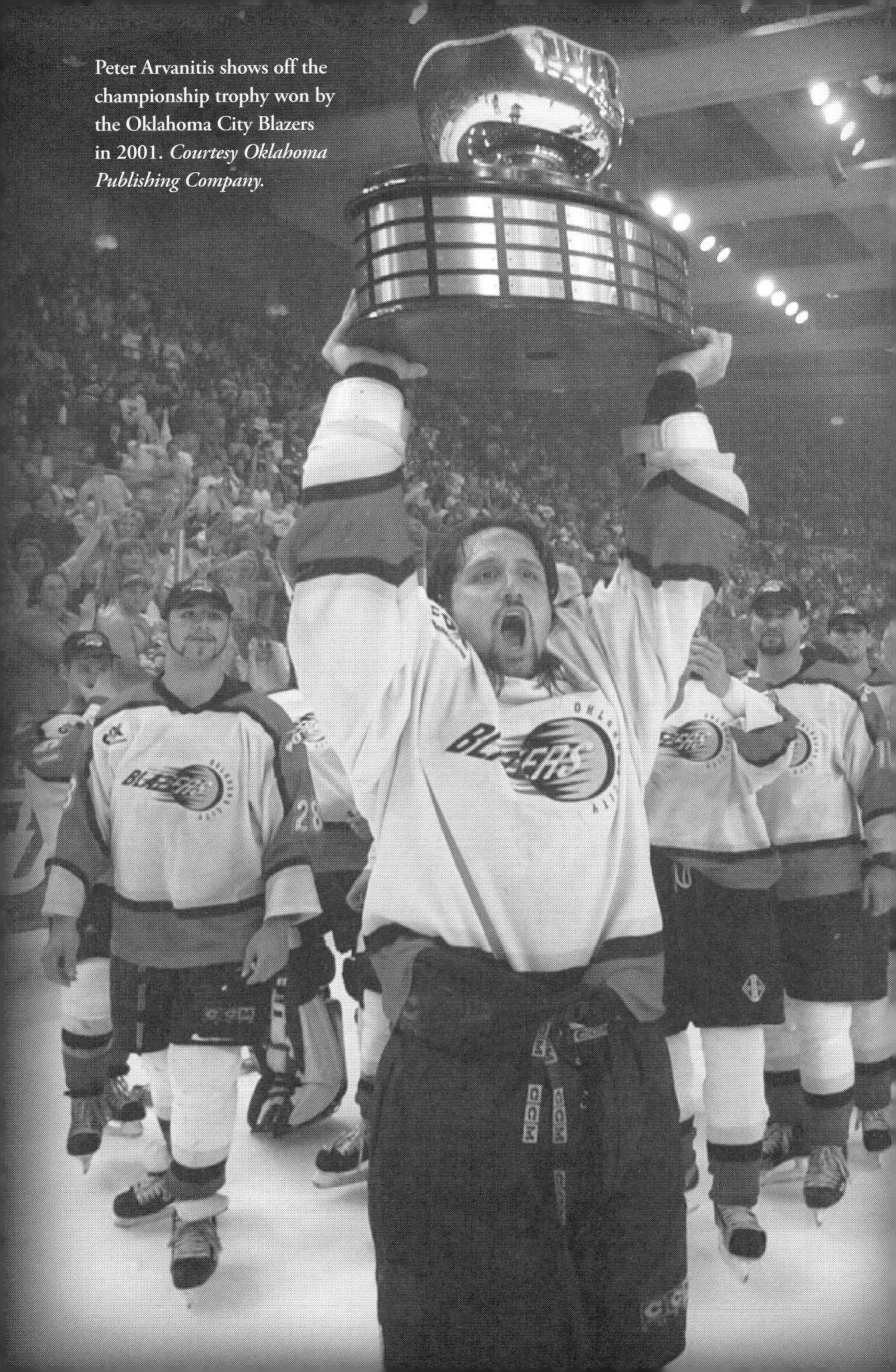

Peter Arvanitis shows off the championship trophy won by the Oklahoma City Blazers in 2001. *Courtesy Oklahoma Publishing Company.*

Sixteen

PUCKS AND LOBS

THE ROAD TO BOB'S INVOLVEMENT AS A SPORTS FRANCHISE owner was pure happenstance. Their love of ranching, horses, and cattle brought Bob together with Oklahoma City Blazers' hockey coach Doug Sauter. The two men had never met when Sauter just happened to appear at Bob's ranch. Sauter, who became coach of the Blazers in 199 i, missed his own off-season ranching operation in Canada.

Bob and Sauter became friends Sauter was instrumental in helping Bob buy his first Clydesdale horses in Canada. In 1999, when the future of the Oklahoma City Blazers' minor league franchise was in question, Sauter and Blazers' general manager Brad Lund asked Bob to think about purchasing the team.

Bob never really had been a hockey fan. In fact, he had been to only three hockey games in his life—and two of those were bad experiences. Years before, he and Nedra had attended a National Hockey League game in Seattle when a nearby patron spilled beer down the back of Nedra's neck. On a business trip to Houston, Bob attended a hockey game with his local Express office manager. Fans who were drinking heavily started a fight and Bob's manager took off his shoe and hit one of them in the head. The manager and Bob were asked to leave.[1]

As a gesture to Sauter, however, Bob agreed to talk to Blazers' minority owner and general manager Brad Lund. Even though he was just 34, Lund had directed operations of the Oklahoma City Cavalry of the Continental Basketball Association from 1990 to 1992. When the Central Hockey League returned a team, the Blazers, to Oklahoma City in 1992, Lund became general manager.

There was talk that the city council of Oklahoma City was interested in bringing the Kansas City Blades, a Triple-A hockey franchise to Oklahoma City. Sauter and Lund believed the Blazers' presence in the Double-A Central Hockey League was healthy for Oklahoma City and that losing the Blazers for a Triple-A team that had lost money in Kansas City, Missouri, was not the right decision for the sports future of Oklahoma City.[2]

Sauter also believed it was unfair to deprive loyal Blazers hockey fans of their team. The Blazers had been one of the few minor league hockey franchises in the nation to make money or break even, and the team had excelled in the Central Hockey League. The Blazers won several championships and always were competitive. Some political observers had suggested that Blazers fans had formed a significant core of supporters of the MAPs project, a citywide development package of which a new 20,000-seat arena was the most costly item.[3]

After several visits with Lund, Bob looked over the financial statements of the Blazers and talked to majority owner Horn Chen, a Chicago businessman, who was seldom seen in Oklahoma City. The out-of-state ownership was one reason city fathers, including Oklahoma City Mayor Kirk Humphreys, were interested in an International Hockey League franchise such as Kansas City. Many observers believed hockey would be the first major league franchise that Oklahoma City could attract and that moving up to a level just below the National Hockey League would be beneficial.[4]

Left to right, Bob Funk, Doug Sauter, and Brad Lund. When Bob bought the Oklahoma City Blazers, he originally talked to Lund as a favor to his ranching buddy, Sauter. *Courtesy David Allen.*

However, Lund had done his homework on the financial position of both the Blades and the International Hockey League. There was no doubt both were having financial problems. As the Oklahoma City city council began considering whether or not to extend the Blazers' lease on the Myriad Convention Center, the site of the team's games, owner Chen came to Oklahoma City and met with Bob and Lund.

Officials knew how Oklahoma City hockey fans felt about losing their Blazers. Oklahoma City annually led the Central Hockey League in attendance. The mayor and city council received a large amount of input from fans, and nearly 100

Bob with longtime radio voice of the Oklahoma City Blazers hockey team John Brooks, left. *Courtesy David Allen.*

percent of them wanted to keep the Blazers. A few irate fans wanted to throw tomatoes at Mayor Humphreys for considering the idea of dumping the Blazers in favor of the Kansas City team.[5]

On the eve of a major meeting with city officials, Chen asked Bob if he could use his name as a supporter of the idea of keeping the Blazers in Oklahoma City. Instead of just allowing his name to be used, Bob and Express Personnel chief operating officer Dave Gillogly headed to city hall with Chen and Lund to talk about the future of the Blazers.

Chen offered Bob a piece of the ownership of the team. By this time, Bob was convinced that Oklahoma City deserved to keep the Blazers. He borrowed the money and bought full ownership of the team and gave his friend Sauter a lifetime contract. However, Bob, Lund, and Sauter still had a hurdle to overcome.

The city government of Oklahoma City was still talking to Kansas City Blades' owner Dan DeVos. In an editorial titled "Fire on Ice," *The Daily Oklahoman* discussed both sides of the war to put a hockey team on ice at the proposed new downtown arena that eventually was built and named the Ford Center.[6]

On one hand, the city council considered the 6,000 to 8,000 loyal Blazers' fans who loved the hometown atmosphere created by Lund and his management team. The other option was to cater to the Kansas City Blades or a new proposal that might give Oklahoma City the top farm team of the National Hockey League's Dallas Stars. That idea might send higher quality hockey players to Oklahoma City, but Blazers' fans did not care.[7]

In a war of dueling press releases, the Blazers had the edge in public relations. *The Daily Oklahoman,* while not taking sides in the battle, admitted that "Funk would be good for the Blazers and the city." The editorial also gave Lund the credit for the success of the team, "The Blazers have a hometown feel, but that's because of the work of General Manager Brad Lund and his homegrown staff."[8]

Bob held news conferences during the time the city council was considering which direction to proceed. Early in January, 2000, Mayor Humphreys told reporters that Oklahoma City hockey fans would pay 95 percent more for tickets if an International Hockey League franchise replaced the Blazers.[9]

A key player in helping the city council make its decision was City Manager Glenn Deck, who compiled massive records on everything from ticket prices to projected revenues of selling souvenirs to hockey fans at the new arena scheduled to open in late 2002.

In the end, Deck suggested to the nine-member city council that the Blazers' lease be extended and that any idea of attracting a AAA hockey franchise to Oklahoma City be put on hold indefinitely. Deck cited fan support, favorable profit margins, and proposed lease terms. Deck was troubled by the Kansas City demand for 35 percent of profits from naming rights to the new arena, 40 percent of the concessions income, and a permanent share of advertising. It was too much of a price to pay for Oklahoma City to move closer to becoming a major league sports city.[10]

Deck's recommendations were presented to the council before a packed chamber filled with Blazers' fans and players. Blazers' winger Peter Arvanitis told the council that fans in Oklahoma City were the best in the world and that he and his fellow players were honored to play in Oklahoma City.[11]

The city council unanimously accepted Deck's recommendations but extended the Blazers' lease for only three years. As far as Bob was concerned, the length of the lease was the only disappointing part of the council's decision.[12] Later in 2000, the city council extended the lease to five years, with an option for another two years. In 2004, the council extended the Blazers' deal until 2014.

The Blazers returned the compliment to the city council. Their fans bought season tickets in record numbers, and the Oklahoma City hockey team ranked in the top five in attendance among the 106 minor league hockey teams in the nation.

In 2001, the Blazers made nearly a clean sweep in the Central Hockey League. They had the league's most valuable player, Joe Burton, top goaltender, Brant Nicklin, and playoff most valuable player, Rod Branch. The Blazers won the regular season title and clinched the Ray Miran Cup championship. They also led minor league hockey in attendance. John Rohde wrote in *The*

Bob uses his position as owner of the Oklahoma City Blazers to benefit local charities and organizations. Players such as Rod Butler, left, autograph their jerseys which have been auctioned to raise money. Young Blazer fan Corbin Campbell, right, gratefully accepted the player's jersey on the ice following the game.

Bob and the 2001
Central Hockey League
champion Oklahoma City
Blazers. *Courtesy David Allen.*

Daily Oklahoman, "You can rest easy about coach Doug Sauter. The adopted Okie from Fairlight, Saskatchewan, said he will return next year, and the next, and the next...Beneath all that facial hair sits a smile as wide as Canada."[13]

Newspaper columnist Berry Tramel called the relationship of Bob and Sauter unusual. Tramel wrote, "It is a strange mix that has paid big for Oklahoma City. They met through their love of horses; the conservative Baptist businessman and the flamboyant Canadian coach." Tramel continued, "Funk laughs long at the question of his friendship with Sauter, then tells the story of how Funk bans the sale of alcohol at the cattle sales at his Piedmont ranch. Sauter responded, 'I'll put up a sinner's tent across the road, sell beer, and I'll make more money than you do.'"[14]

The significant contributions Bob made by keeping the Blazers viable in Oklahoma City was summarized by long-time sportswriter Bob Hersom who covered hockey in 2003 for the first time in 30 years of covering other sports. Hersom wrote:

> Blazers owner Bob Funk is one of the most respected people in the state, on a personal and professional level. And like I told him one time, I've had cars that cost less than that rich looking leather jacket he wears. Express Sports CEO Brad Lund reminds me that someone in history, probably Napoleon, was nicknamed "The Little General." Lund is The Little Genius of local sports marketing...Hockey is a grand game.[15]

In December, 2000, Bob formed Express Sports to operate the Blazers and any other sports ventures that came his way. Lund became chief executive officer of the new corporation as Bob and Lund began thinking about other sports properties.

Bob scored a major sports coup in 2002 when he signed commitment papers to bring Davis Cup tennis matches to

Oklahoma City. Bob put up the required $200,000 to entice the United States Tennis Association to bring the best in tennis to the Myriad Arena, newly renamed the Cox Business Services Convention Center.[16]

Bob had long supported professional tennis in Oklahoma City. For years, Express Personnel was a major corporate sponsor of the annual IGA Tennis Classic. The women's tennis tournament drew large crowds and increased the popularity of tennis in Oklahoma City. However, women's tour financial problems ended the Oklahoma City visit in 2000.

The first round of the Davis Cup competition being played in Oklahoma City was big news to tennis fans. "Next to a major championship," Brad Lund said, "it's the biggest thing you can get."[17]

Berry Tramel recognized Bob's commitment to professional tennis in Oklahoma City:

Bob Funk delivered. We've had the PGA and March Madness and the routine Oklahoma football epic. But Davis Cup brings international intrigue. We've seen Fred Couples and Nebraska plenty...

We've had Monica Seles and Venus Williams serve on our tennis courts, but Davis Cup adds equal star power, with the patriotism kicker. Warhorse Pete Sampras and young stud Andy Roddick, with American flags flapping over the Myriad on a February weekend. The CBA All-Star Game this ain't.

Davis Cup, even the first round, is tennis with a rock 'n roll beat. A stale individual game is juiced by a team concept. The stodgy warnings at the IGA Classic—"Quiet please;" "Take a seat; any seat will do"—give way to chants of "USA! USA!"[18]

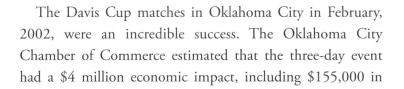

The Davis Cup matches in Oklahoma City in February, 2002, were an incredible success. The Oklahoma City Chamber of Commerce estimated that the three-day event had a $4 million economic impact, including $155,000 in sales tax revenue. More than 20,000 tickets were sold to spectators to watch the world's best tennis players from 16 countries. The impact was nearly twice the positive effect that the first round had on Winston-Salem, North Carolina, the year before.[19]

The Davis Cup is referred to as the "Olympics of Tennis." The actual attendance of 18,056 fans set an American record for the first round of Davis Cup competition. Fans came from 29 states. Oklahoma Governor Frank Keating said, "The Davis

Nedra and Bob are honored for bringing the Davis Cup matches to Oklahoma City. *Courtesy David Allen.*

Cup brought people from all over the country to see what Oklahoma City has done. The hotels were filled. The restaurants were filled. It was a significant boost to our economy."[20]

Other sports ideas came across the desks of Brad Lund and Bob. They had the opportunity to review proposals for major league soccer and tennis and golf events. Express Sports had become a major league player in the future of sports in Oklahoma City.

ABOVE: Bob posed with members of the American Davis Cup tennis team in 2002 when the first round was played in Oklahoma City. Behind Bob is Bobby Funk. *Courtesy David Allen.*

RIGHT: Brad Lund, chief executive officer of Express Sports, was elated with the economic jolt Oklahoma City received from the Davis Cup matches in 2002. *Courtesy Oklahoma Publishing Company.*

Bob used his corporate entity, Express Sports, to promote professional sports in Oklahoma. *Courtesy Oklahoma Publishing Company.*

Seventeen

SULTAN OF SPORTS

WITH SEVERAL YEARS OF SUCCESSFUL OWNERSHIP
of the Oklahoma City Blazers under his belt, Bob was approached
in 2003 about buying the Oklahoma RedHawks, the AAA farm
club of the Texas Rangers. The RedHawks played in the new
SBC Bricktown Ballpark, recognized as one of America's finest
minor league baseball stadiums.

The RedHawks, a member of the Pacific Coast League, were
successors to the 89ers and Indians who had thrilled Oklahoma
City baseball fans for decades. The club was owned by Gaylord
Entertainment Company which had purchased the franchise for
$8 million from New York art dealer Jeffrey Loria after the 1993
season. Loria later bought the major league Florida Marlins.[1]

Bob's partners in buying the RedHawks in July, 2003, were
State Senator Scott Pruitt of Broken Arrow, Oklahoma, and
Dave Gillogly. Pruitt, an avid baseball fan, came to Bob with
news that an out-of-state prospective buyer was close to purchasing the team. Recognizing the importance of local ownership
in sports properties, Bob bought 51 percent ownership in the
team. Pruitt, a 25 percent owner, was originally from Kentucky
and had played baseball for the University of Kentucky. He later
graduated from the University of Tulsa law school.[2]

ABOVE: State Senator Scott Pruitt, left, and Bob celebrate their new ownership of the Oklahoma RedHawks minor league baseball franchisse. *Courtesy
Oklahoma Publishing Company.*

RIGHT: During the first year of Bob's ownership of the Oklahoma RedHawks,
the team had the second highest annual attendance since the opening of the
SBC Bricktown Ballpark. *Courtesy Oklahoma Publishing Company.*

Bob's entry into the limelight of owning a baseball franchise was applauded by Berry Tramel in *The Daily Oklahoman,* "Funk didn't enter sports to make money. He bought the Blazers to save a pal, coach Doug Sauter, whose franchise was being usurped by another league. He didn't buy the RedHawks to make money, because minor-league baseball is no cash cow."[3]

"Bob's an ideal sports owner," Brad Lund said, "because he's got passion." It was no secret that Bob bought the RedHawks to help his community maintain local ownership and local pride in the team.

After the sale was announced, Bob said, "The local ownership issue is what drove us to do this so rapidly. We really did not want to see an outside entity that may not have as much interest in the future of our city and state."[4]

Bob was an unusual baseball team owner in another way. Lund said, "He wants to have the best attendance and best fireworks show. But he also likes to have fun. He is actually a kid, not a rich kid playing with big toys, but a kid who likes hanging around the locker room and going to new places and feeling a part of something special."[5]

By November, 2003, the Pacific Coast League had approved the RedHawks sale. After final negotiations, Bob and Pruitt owned 88 percent of the team. Former Express Personnel Chief Operating Officer Dave Gillogly and Pruitt's law partner, Ken Wagner of Tulsa, rounded out the leadership of Oklahoma Baseball Club, LLC, the entity that claimed ownership of the RedHawks. The corporation owned 95 percent of the ball club.[6]

Pruitt became the managing general partner of the RedHawks. Pacific Coast League president Branch Rickey called the purchase of the RedHawks by Bob and his partners "another step forward for baseball in Oklahoma City."[7]

The new ownership began plans to celebrate the centennial anniversary of professional baseball in Oklahoma City. The first team was fielded in 1904. Pruitt said, "We need to create a festive atmosphere. We want people, when they leave the ballpark to say, 'We had a great time, and by the way, did we win or lose?'" The RedHawks offered more promotions and more options and more flexibility in ticket packages, without an increase in ticket prices.[8]

When the 2004 season began, the RedHawks took the field with new uniforms. Fans enjoyed several new food items including Krispy Kreme donuts and Blue Bell ice cream. A new audio system was installed in the stadium, and food vendors sold peanuts and almonds that were roasted on the ball park concourse. Free scorecards and pencils were given to fans and new carpet was installed on the third level. To cater to down-town businessmen, one-fourth of the RedHawks' games were scheduled to begin in the morning or shortly after noon.[9]

Co-owner Pruitt said, "We are trying to create raving fans. We want them to rave about the ballpark and the service and the food. We want to make sure their experience from the beginning of the game to the end of the game is outstanding."[10]

The innovations and hard work paid off. In Bob's second year as primary owner of the team, all previous attendance records were broken.

Bob was honored for his contributions to sports in 2004 when he received the Abe Lemons/Paul Hansen Award for Sports Excellence from Oklahoma City University. Former Oklahoma Congressman J.C. Watts called Bob "the ultimate sports supporter" in presenting the award.[11]

Bob had plenty to relish about his first year as owner of the RedHawks. The team drew 474,206 fans, the second-highest total in the history of professional baseball in Oklahoma City. The only higher attendance year was in 1998, the first year Bricktown Ballpark opened. On the field, the RedHawks won 81 games during the regular season and coasted to the Pacific Coast League's Eastern Division title.[12]

Bob sat down with *The Daily Oklahoman* sportswriter Bob Hersom and talked about the future of sports in Oklahoma. In a column titled, "Funk—the Sultan of Sports," Hersom related Bob's promise that he would look at any sporting event that would be beneficial to Oklahoma City, including National Basketball Association and National Hockey League teams. He also talked about sponsoring tennis and rodeo events. Hersom called Bob "the most influential person in Oklahoma professional sports."[13]

In 2005, when the New Orleans Hornets began to play their National Basketball Association season at the Ford Center of Oklahoma City because of Hurricane Katrina's devastation of New Orleans, Bob's bold predictions about Oklahoma City being able to host a major league sport came true. Two years before, in a newspaper interview, Bob said, "I believe that the first major league team that comes to Oklahoma will be successful. If we can find 25 or 30 companies who will provide a lot of support, it will succeed because Oklahomans take a lot of pride in themselves."[14]

Bob was right. Oklahoma City leaders and corporate citizens shared risks and rewards and made possible professional basketball for Oklahoma City fans who responded in record numbers. Sellout crowds cheered the Hornets to a successful season in 2005-2006. Bob cooperated by moving several Blazers' hockey games that conflicted with Hornets' basketball games from the Ford Center to the Cox Convention Center across the street.

Oklahoma City Mayor Mick Cornett wanted the Blazers' interest to be addressed. He said, "We've talked to Brad Lund and Bob Funk, and they are on board. They want it to happen. But they also don't want to be negatively impacted."[15] The Blazers were negatively impacted, especially when their games were played on the same nights as Hornets' games. However, Bob, being the community-spirited leader that he is, ignored the problems and continued to support major league basketball in Oklahoma City.[16]

In addition to hockey, baseball, and tennis, Bob launched into the world of professional rodeo competition in 2003. Express Sports formed a marketing partnership in which the company sponsored a bull riding team field by Professional Bull Riders, Inc. (PBR). Oklahoma bull riders Jody Newberry of Ada, Corey Navarre of Weatherford, and Luke Young of Wright

City entered an international competition in Connecticut carrying the Express banner. The company gained national publicity because more than 100 million viewers tune in each year to the PBR on NBC television.[17]

In 2004, PBR and Express Sports, along with the Tulsa Oilers, sponsored the first ever PBR bull-riding tour stop in Tulsa. It was part of a three-year arrangement between PBR and Express Sports to promote the Built Ford Tough Series, which featured outstanding bull riders at events across the country. Bob said, "When it became clear that Tulsa had a chance to obtain the premier bull riding tour, we stepped in and agreed to co-promote the event with the PBR."[18]

Whether it's bull riding, hockey, soccer, golf, tennis, or baseball, Bob's involvement is never about making money—it is about promoting events that bring quality sporting entertainment to Oklahoma, and adds to the pride that he feels as one who has adopted Oklahoma as his home.

Bob, center, talks with professional bull riders Corey Navarre, left, and Jody Newberry at Express Headquarters in Oklahoma City. *Courtesy Oklahoma Publishing Company.*

Bob with former Polish President
Lech Walesa who won the Nobel
Peace Prize in 1983.

Eighteen

PUBLIC SERVICE

WHEN BOB IS NOT BEHIND HIS DESK at Express Personnel, watching his hockey team on the ice, or working with his cattle or Clydesdales, he is in the public eye. As his business grew, city and national groups and universities recognized his accomplishments.

In 1995, Bob was awarded an honorary doctorate of public service from Seattle Pacific University. An honorary doctorate of law was presented to him by Oklahoma Baptist University in 2000, and an honorary doctorate of law was presented by Southern Nazarene University in 2001.[1]

Bob served on the board of the International Franchising Association (IFA). He was the IFA's Entrepreneur of the Year in 2000 and was named as a trustee of IFA's Educational Foundation. Bob was inducted into three halls of fame—the Sales and Marketing Executives International Hall of Fame, the National Association of Personnel Services Hall of Fame, and the National Stockman's Hall of Fame.[2]

As an outgrowth of his involvement at First Baptist Church in Piedmont, Bob was named to the board of trustees at Oklahoma Baptist University (OBU) in Shawnee, Oklahoma. He also served as chairman of the OBU Board of Trustees, chairman of the OBU Business Affairs Committee, and is a lifetime member of the OBU President's Council. He was a member of the Business Advisory Council for Oklahoma Christian University of Science and Arts in Oklahoma City.[3]

Bob was elated with the election of Oklahoma Republican Governor Frank Keating in 1994. Bob became active in calling for pro-business reforms in state government. He and Nedra became close friends with Governor Keating and First Lady Cathy Keating. When the First Lady launched a major effort to renovate the Oklahoma governor's mansion, Bob and Nedra served as co-chairmen of the effort to raise private monies to build a visitor's center at the mansion. The result was the construction of the much-used Phillips Pavilion, built immediately behind the governor's mansion.[4]

The Funks and Keatings took many trips together. The First Lady had her first successful elk hunt with the Funks. Bob enjoyed poking fun at Governor Keating. After a day of hunting, Bob proposed a toast and handed the governor a glass of what was presumed to be wine. However, Bob, the non-drinking Baptist, had filled the glass with non-alcoholic wine. Not considering the gravity of the moment, Governor Keating took a long sip of the liquid, then promptly spit it back into the glass. Keating said, "It was the worst tasting stuff imaginable." The following year, the Keatings presented the Funks with a re-touched framed photograph of a nineteenth century saloon named the "Dry Saloon at Dry Gulch," the name Keating gave the Funk ranch in New Mexico.[5]

On a more serious note, Bob became the unofficial Santa Claus for worthy projects noted by First Lady Cathy Keating. On many occasions, Mrs. Keating called for Bob's help for people in desperate need. She said, "He wanted no recognition, no publicity. He epitomizes the saying that the true character of

LEFT: Governor Frank and First Lady Cathy Keating declare Bob and Nedra Funk Week in appreciation of the tremendous donations to the Capitol Dome and the Phillips Pavilion.

ABOVE: A dome was added to the Oklahoma State Capitol in 2002. As a tribute to the $1 million contribution from Express, the words "Express Personnel—Bob and Nedra Funk" are carved into the marble that surrounds the inside of the dome. *Courtesy Eric Dabney.*

a man can be judged not by what is done when everyone can see but when no one is looking."[6]

Bob and Nedra's friendship with the Keatings made the Funks a natural contributor to the project to add the long-awaited dome to the State Capitol. Bob and Nedra contributed $1 million to the magnificent addition.

Through the Keatings, Bob became good friends with Archie W. Dunham, the retired chairman of ConocoPhillips, one of the nation's major oil companies. Knowing that Bob and Dunham shared common priorities—God, family, and country—the Keatings arranged a dinner to talk about hunting, fishing, and ranching. From the time they met, the Funks and Dunhams have fished remote streams and lakes in Alaska, hunted elk, bear, and mountain lions at Bob's ranch in New Mexico, and helped raise funds to build new facilities at the Falls Creek Baptist Youth Camp in the Arbuckle Mountains in southern Oklahoma.[7]

In 2002, Bob became chairman of the Oklahoma City Chamber of Commerce. He took seriously the job as the head of the 113-year-old organization that began shortly after the Land Run of 1889. Bob believed Oklahoma was very "saleable" to companies outside the state who should be told of the great Oklahoma work ethic.

He also pledged to help existing businesses succeed. He wanted to make big and small businesses aware of Oklahoma's quality of life, low housing costs, low property tax, low crime rate, moderate traffic, the MAPS projects in Bricktown and downtown Oklahoma City, and the city's inexpensive labor.[8]

Retired General Richard "Dick" Burpee, the president of the Oklahoma City Chamber of Commerce directed the group's day-to-day operations. Of Bob's leadership, Burpee said, "He was a great chairman. Being a businessman, he offered invaluable guidance and oversight but did not micromanage the chamber. He is a people-oriented guy who made sure the people working in the chamber and convention and visitors bureau were treated properly. He was very approachable, and I could contact him on any issue, any time."[9]

Bob's year at the helm of the chamber was challenging because the country was coming out of a mild recession. Burpee remembered, "Investors in the chamber were more guarded in their contributions." The atmosphere caused Bob to give higher than normal attention to fundraising.[10]

Bob worked tirelessly for the economic development of Oklahoma City. He helped develop the Silver Springs Crossing retail center and the Commerce Park office center. He was the leader in attracting Quad Graphics Printing Company to Oklahoma City after a substantial delay due to the recession. Quad Graphics is one of the largest privately-owned printing companies in the world. Once the printing plant was completed, 350 new jobs were added to the Oklahoma City economy. The company also announced plans to expand their Oklahoma City plant to one-million square feet.[11]

Bob led the recruitment of the Johnson Controls Company plant that employed 350 people manufacturing headliners for automobiles. He was open in his support for the city giving economic incentives to lure Bass Pro Shops to the Bricktown area. Bob understood the controversy of giving incentives to some businesses but wanted to build the friendliest possible environment for all business decision makers. He was in favor of using incentives to compete with neighboring states.[12]

As chamber chairman, Bob led the campaign for a $50 million Oklahoma County bond issue to clear encroachment zones around Tinker Air Force Base in preparation for the 2005 Base Realignment and Closure Commission. The bond issue passed with more than 72.2 percent voter approval, the highest percentage of any bond issue in the history of the county. The approval was an important element of the chamber working to keep Tinker Air Force Base, the state's largest employer, viable.[13]

Bob became a spokesman for employers who believed Oklahoma's workers' compensation insurance system needed to be reformed. In a guest editorial in *The Daily Oklahoman,* Bob wrote:

ABOVE: Bob speaks at the annual State of the City luncheon at the Myriad Convention Center on January 29, 2002. *Courtesy Oklahoma Publishing Company.*

RIGHT: Following his year as chairman of the Oklahoma City Chamber of Commerce, Bob, left, was succeeded in the post by Burns Hargis. *Courtesy Oklahoma Publishing Company.*

Workers' comp is basically an insurance program to protect people who get hurt on the job. It's supposed to pay their medical costs and replace their pay with disability income while they heal, and sustain them with larger awards in cases of permanent disability that prevents them from returning to work.

It's not a lawyer enrichment program or a playground for fraud artists, but all too often that's what is has become under our state's current system. Let's fix it now and get Oklahoma moving into the 21st century.[14]

Bob cited that Express Personnel's workers' compensation costs were higher in Oklahoma than in other states in which the company operated. Bob joined the effort by a group called Oklahomans for Workers' Compensation Reform, which

announced intentions to fund an initiative petition drive to make reforms in workers' compensation unless the Oklahoma legislature acted. Bob and John Brock, a Tulsa businessman, were named co-chairmen of the group which touted the idea that an administrative system would provide a better benefits delivery system to injured workers than the existing court system.[15]

The legislature heeded the call for workers' compensation reform from Bob, the Oklahoma State Chamber of Commerce, Governor Brad Henry, and many business leaders. In 2005, the legislature passed the most sweeping reform in state history, a move that is expected to save employers millions of dollars in insurance premiums in the future.[16]

After the bill passed, Oklahomans for Workers' Compensation Reform dropped its plan for an initiative petition drive, based upon estimates that the new law would ultimately save Oklahoma businesses $120 million a year.[17]

In 2004, Bob was appointed chairman of the Federal Reserve Bank of Kansas City (FRBKC). He had served on the bank's Oklahoma City branch board of directors.

The Federal Reserve System was created by Congress in 1913, following an era marked by financial panics and economic depressions. The goal of the system is to stabilize the economy. The Federal Reserve is a bank for banks, a bank for the federal government, and a regulator of banks in the United States. The Federal Reserve provides currency to local banks, oversees proposed mergers of banks, and assures consumers they receive fair treatment under banking and privacy laws.[18]

Bob had long known the importance of the Federal Reserve System in setting monetary policy and influencing the growth of money and credit in the national economy. When the supply of money grew too rapidly in relation to businesses' ability to

Bob, right, with Federal Reserve Chairman Alan Greenspan. Bob had great faith in Greenspan's wisdom in directing the American economy. In 2007, Bob was elected as chairman of the chairmen of the Federal Reserve Board.

produce goods and services, inflation was the result. Too little growth in the money supply can lead to recession and unemployment. The Federal Reserve does a balancing act to try to avoid either of these extremes.[19]

The Federal Reserve Bank of Kansas City serves banking institutions and the public in Oklahoma, Colorado, Kansas, Nebraska, Wyoming, northern New Mexico, and western Missouri. It is known as the Tenth Federal Reserve District with branches located in Denver, Colorado, Oklahoma City, and Omaha, Nebraska.[20]

Bob accepted the prestigious position as chairman of all chairmen nationwide of the Federal Reserve Bank of Kansas City board with the intent of doing his best to make right decisions for the economy. He related his own experiences to fellow board members and Alan Greenspan, former chairman of the Federal Reserve Board of Governors. Greenspan was considered by many to be the most powerful man in the world because his remarks often sent the stock market up or down.

Thomas M. Hoening, president of the FRBKC, called Bob "intuitive" about the Federal Reserve's mission. "Without question," Hoening said, "Bob is one of the busiest members of the board but he makes all the meetings and is always

Left to right, Bill Stoller, Desert Storm hero General Norman Schwarzkopf, and Bob.

prepared. He has taken on the difficult responsibility as board chairman with the highest degree of integrity. He consistently demonstrates that he has the best interest of the Federal Reserve, the country, and just as importantly, the Bank's employees, in mind as he works with other directors on these challenging decisions."[21]

Bob's position on the Federal Reserve Bank board gave him an opportunity to speak out on economic issues. When the dollar dropped to an all-time low against the euro in December, 2004, Bob was optimistic that a soft dollar could boost exports as stronger foreign currencies bought more American goods. Even though some economists feared the worst from a soft dollar, Bob said, "It could be welcome news for us over the short term."[22]

Bob and Nedra's philosophy always has been to give back to their church, community, state, and nation. In addition to supporting their local church, they have contributed significantly to colleges and universities, local schools, Oklahoma City's Allied Arts, and their hometown of Piedmont, where they donated land to build a public library.

In 2004, the Funks made a multi-million dollar contribution for the renovation of the football stadium at Oklahoma State University (OSU). Newspapers guessed at the amount of the gift but called it second in size only to the contribution of oilman Boone Pickens for whom the stadium is named. The Funks made the contribution to OSU because of Bob's agricultural background and OSU's commitment to agriculture. His family was also a consideration. Bob's son-in-law, Chris Bridges, attended OSU, and Bob admitted that Chris was influential in the decision.

The Funks greatly assisted the Boy Scouts of America when they purchased the Atmore Ranch in New Mexico. Bob never intended to own a ranch in that state, but the Boy Scouts needed someone to buy the ranch in order to preserve it. Millions of Boy Scouts spent summer camp at the neighboring Philmont Scout Ranch that was given to the Boy Scouts of America by Tulsa, Oklahoma, oilman Waite Phillips decades before. The Atmore Ranch, consisting of 2,200 acres, basically was in the middle of the Philmont Ranch area and provided easy access to much of Philmont's acreage.[23]

Bob's cousin, Ed Pease, was instrumental in showing Bob and Nedra the New Mexico property. Pease was a member of the national Boy Scouts board and served on the committee that managed the Philmont Scout Ranch. Pease and others were concerned that Boy Scouts' access to their property would be greatly impaired if someone friendly did not buy the Atmore Ranch. Pease said, "To get from the south part of the Philmont Ranch to the north side, you must go through the Atmore Ranch or you have some serious climbing over mountains."[24]

When Bob was looking at the Atmore Ranch, he learned that a developer was interested in buying the property, selling lots, paving streets, and eliminating the Boy Scouts' access. As a favor to the Boy Scouts, Bob purchased the ranch so generations of boys could use his property to gain access to the wilderness they had been using for 60 years.[25]

Bob has guided Express Personnel into commitments to several major charities. The American Heart Association is the leader in the fight against heart disease and strokes that kill one million Americans each year. Bob and Nedra have a personal interest in American Heart Association programs. Their daughter, Julie, suffered a cardiac arrest at age 22. Julie's gratitude to her rescuers prompted her involvement in lobbying the legislature to pass laws that provide defibrillators in public places and CPR training and instruction in the use of defibrillators in emergencies.[26]

The Children's Miracle Network has been the primary focus of Express Personnel's national philanthropic effort since 1991. The organization provides medical resources, research, and other programs to benefit children in more than 170 hospitals in North America. Express, as a national Children's Miracle Network sponsor, has contributed nearly $3 million to the organization.[27]

When Express Personnel expanded its operations into South Africa in 1998, the company recognized the over-whelming problems of poverty and inequities among the country's diverse population. Express contributed substantially to Project Lupesi to teach modern life skills to future generations of rural and tribal Africans. The project includes components of education and medical help, along with developing infrastructure such as water and electrical systems, agricultural initiatives, and game preserves. Bob said, "We want to give Africans the tools necessary to find solutions to their many needs."[28]

Project Lupesi is named for the remote village of Lupesi, seven hours outside Pretoria, South Africa. Lupesi, with its thatched mud huts and dung rondavaals, is home to several thousand people, including more than 800 students and 16 teachers. Express provided money to build three classrooms and sent a professional contractor to the village to teach residents how to make cinder blocks, drive nails, erect a frame, and finally attach the roof to the buildings. Express is hopeful that the skills learned will make life better for the village hidden from the modern world.[29]

Express also has provided residents of Lupesi with a barren crèche, or daycare center, with toys and supplies, and helped stock the local medical clinic with medicines and supplies. Express has plans to expand its African effort by building schools in other villages.

Express, with 10 offices in South Africa as of 2007, is committed to helping that nation. Linda Haneborg said, "The giving back to people in South Africa was truly the Express family in action. No matter what part of the globe, we are there to help."[30]

While Bob continued his active involvement in Express, Nedra branched out into a different arena. After a dozen years of running the accounting side of a growing Express Personnel, Nedra trained her successor, Andi Boutwell, a certified public accountant, and launched her own business in 1998. She founded Arden and Associates, a decorating firm. Arden is Nedra spelled backward.[31]

For years, Nedra was in charge of decorating new Express offices and became familiar with art and interior decorating companies. She developed a good taste for decorating. She hired art consultant Cindy Bench from a company she had done business with and formed Arden.

Nedra oversaw the construction of a large building in the business section of Piedmont. From the site, Arden designs frames for art and provides other interior decorating services. Arden focuses on artwork ordered by designers for commercial businesses. Six sales representatives call on design firms across the country.

The first year Arden was in business, the company provided framed artwork for new and remodeled Hard Rock Café locations. The last Hard Rock that Arden provided artwork for was in Cairo, Egypt.[32]

In 2006, Arden was involved in refurbishing the historic Skirvin Hotel in downtown Oklahoma City. The state's oldest existing hotel was built in 1911, but closed in 1988. It reopened in 2007 as the Skirvin Hilton Hotel, a showplace that remains on the National Register of Historic Places.[33]

Founder Nedra Funk started Arden & Associates in 1998 as a result of being an avid art collector. Arden boasts a 25,000-square-foot manufacturing facility and showroom in the heart of Oklahoma. Arden is a unique wholesale art resource for all hospitality, healthcare, corporate, and commercial projects.

Bob and Nedra's grandchildren, Bowen James, left, and Bailey Ruth. Bowen and Bailey's mother, Julie Funk Bridges, says of her father "His greatest legacy will be that he cares for others so much. He truly believes that life is not about one's self, it is about others."

Nineteen

GIVING HOPE

Our greatest good—and what we least can spare—is hope.

—Abraham Cowley

The day the Lord created hope was probably the same day he created spring.

—Bern Williams

We judge of man's wisdom by his hope.

—Ralph Waldo Emerson

Hope is necessary in every condition. The miseries of poverty, sickness, and captivity would, without this comfort, be insupportable.

—William Shakespeare

To people close to Bob, he has not changed much since the days when he was living from paycheck to paycheck. His very existence is surrounded by his burning desire to give others hope. His businesses have been very successful—but his personal goals have never veered from the well-worn path. He grew up in humble surroundings and has never forgotten the value system he learned as a child. He said, "It's okay to have things and money, but they have no real meaning."[1]

Merv Hackney, a pharmacist who has joined Bob in everything from oil and gas deals to cattle feed lot operations, said, "He's still a nice guy. When he talks to me, he's still the Bob Funk I knew 35 years ago—a practicing Christian who loves people and wants to help them."[2]

Bob knows all things on earth are temporal. After he was named Ernst & Young Entrepreneur of the Year in 2005, he humbly said, "I'm not sure I'm that successful. You're only as successful as the last person you helped."[3]

"Hope is what has kept Bob going all these years," Bill Stoller said, "He cares a lot about other people. Using the company to help others around the world is a priority in his life."[4]

Bob's nephew, Cory Benton, sees Bob as an encouraging mentor. He said, "There was a time during college when I was tired and burned out—I was on the verge of quitting. But it was Uncle Bob's encouragement that kept me going." Benton has not only been Bob's student professionally at Express, he has learned more important principles. "The most important things of life that you see in Uncle Bob are his values for God and people. His desire to assist in the development of others, both individually and professionally, is what I believe to be his defining quality."[5]

There are many people who can attest to the fact that Bob is a man of his word. Kingfisher, Oklahoma, attorney Paul Schulte related the story of a client who walked into his office in 1997 and said Bob had promised to help buy him a ranch. Schulte was skeptical when Leroy Richardson said he had nothing in writing from Bob but his word. Richardson had helped Bob add to his Express Ranches acreage for years and Bob had, with a handshake, made the promise to help him purchase his own ranching operation. [6]

Within a few weeks, Bob made good on his word and provided much of the money for Richardson to purchase a 1,200-acre ranch in Coal County, Oklahoma. Schulte said, "I was flabbergasted to see someone come through on such a huge promise."[7]

Cathy Keating, former First Lady of Oklahoma and a member of the Express Personnel Board of Directors, said, "Bob is a brilliant risk-taker with big dreams. He always puts people first. His footprints in the Oklahoma landscape will be permanently emblazoned in our buildings, our history books, and our hearts."[8]

Express Vice President Scott Davis said Bob's resolve and focus remains the same today as it was in the early days of the company. Davis said, "The more things change, the more they stay the same. While issues come and go, Bob still wants every office to become No. 1 in the market and the company to be the biggest in the world."[9]

Former Oklahoma Governor George Nigh, a long-time advisor to Bob and his companies, said the success of Express Personnel, and Bob's other ventures are due to the combination of his integrity and tenacity. "Without those two qualities," Nigh said, "an upstart company could not have become one of the leading companies in Oklahoma and the nation."[10]

Bob's love of people never pushed him into going public with his company. On the contrary, he is proud of Express Personnel's position as the largest privately-held company in the personnel industry.

Even though Bob is a passionate cattleman and beloved sports team owner, his "calling" is in finding jobs for people who need jobs. Sam Hammons said, "I have seen tears come to his eyes when he talks about helping people meet the basic needs of their families while providing a sense of dignity and self-worth that comes with productive work."[11]

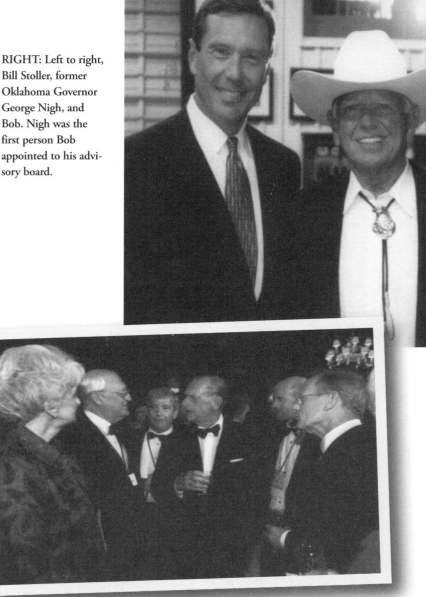

RIGHT: Left to right, Bill Stoller, former Oklahoma Governor George Nigh, and Bob. Nigh was the first person Bob appointed to his advisory board.

ABOVE: Nedra, left, and Bob meet Prince Philip of Great Britain at a 2002 reception at the University of Edinburgh in Scotland. Bob contributed $1 million to the university's library.

Once Bob and Express developer Jerry Baird were in Dyersburg, Tennessee, for the opening of a new Express office when he received a telephone call about the hospitalization of Jerry Scofield, an Express franchisee in Waco, Texas, with a severe prostate cancer problem. Bob canceled the remainder of his schedule and tried desperately to get to Texas. He and Baird drove to Memphis, Tennessee, and booked a flight through Dallas to Waco.[12]

At the hospital, Bob convinced Scofield to travel to a national cancer center for treatment. While Scofield was away, Baird and Mark Tasler helped keep the Express office up and running. Baird remembered, "That is the way Bob has always operated. He puts his people first. He was our leader and showed us the way. If someone needed help, we didn't just call and send a check. We were there in person to help."[13]

Linda Haneborg said, "The basis of our culture at Express is to provide hope for people. Every person who walks into one of our offices will be treated with respect, be given hope, and the best opportunity we can find for them. Bob's leadership engages our souls. We who are fortunate to work with him don't just push buttons and push paper—we push people. We are able to live through the relationships with the people we help."[14]

"I think seeing people succeed gives Bob his biggest thrill in life," said Nikki Sells. "He loves it when someone has had a difficult time but all of a sudden succeeds in a big way. He always wants to hear the stories of success. It validates for him that he has created a monster company that works."[15]

ABOVE: Bob and President George W. Bush. Bob was invited to a small gathering at the home of Senate Majority Leader Bill Frist in February, 2006. At the dinner, President Bush outlined problems that the federal government should address.

RIGHT: Bob and grandson Bowen James, learning the cattle business.

RIGHT: Bob, left, and Reverend Billy Graham, whose simple message of salvation changed young Bobby Funk's life a half century before.

Bob's philosophy of helping people is summarized in Express Personnel's official vision statement:

For many people who have lost their jobs, often through no fault of their own, we provide great hope. Our vision is to help as many people as possible to find jobs and our clients find good people, and to help those clients to make those jobs and those employees even better.

Bob, the "Doctor of Hope," and Nedra. *Courtesy Dr. John Edwards.*

THE NEXT TO THE LAST CHAPTER

If a man's worth is decided by the size of his heart, Uncle Bob's worth cannot be calculated by human standards.

—Cory Benton

Our success begins with Bob Funk. It's not just developing a better way to deliver payroll, it's the culture, it's Bob Funk's culture.

—Linda Haneborg

Helping people—giving hope to people looking for jobs to be able to support their families—has been Bob Funk's life for more than three decades. Along the way, he has had the opportunity to touch the lives of more than two million people.

"Life is all about people," Bob reflects, "it's not about things. As you get older, you realize that the true, lasting friends you make in life are what give you pleasure in your existence later. Friends are more important than anything else if you want to enjoy your later years."[1]

Bob is not so much concerned about the success of today, but what changes he has helped bring about that will affect the future. "The key," he says, "is to do what's right and charge on down the road."[2]

Bob would be the last person to claim his business acumen is totally responsible for the success of Express. Linda Haneborg said, "A whole lot of prayer has gone into the growth of this company."[3] Carol Lane said, "Express reflects Bob's personal belief because we are built on a Christian foundation. He sets the standard for the staff at corporate headquarters, and he expects each one of us to set an example for our franchisees."[4]

Bill Stoller recounts, "It is the essence of the man and his delivery of all the virtues—his faith, his hope, his charity—that sets the stage for all of us."

Bob's faith is demonstrated in an annual prayer breakfast at the company's international leadership conference. Express is one of very few international companies that includes a prayer breakfast into official functions.

Fortunately for many people around the world, the last chapters of Bob's life are yet to be written. He still is active in the daily affairs of the business he co-founded. He has never lost sight of his desire to give hope to others. On any occasion where an audience is gathered, he shares his heart-felt creed:

You can live 40 days without food,
four days without water,
four minutes without air,
but you cannot live four seconds without HOPE!

NOTES

two / Hard Times in King County

1. www.cityofduvall. com, the official website of Duvall, Washington; www.wikipedia. com/cascades.
2. www.historylink. org, containing "Duvall— Thumbnail History."
3. www.en.wikipedia. org/King_county,_ Washington.
4. www.historylink. org.
5. Ibid.
6. Interviews with Robert Allen "Bob" Funk, November and December, 2005, and January 2006, hereafter referred to as Bob Funk interview, Archives, Oklahoma Heritage Association, Oklahoma City, Oklahoma, hereafter referred to as Heritage Archives.
7. Ibid.
8. Ibid.
9. Ibid.
10. Ibid.
11. Interview with Elnora Trim, September 15, 2005, hereafter referred to as Elnora Trim interview, Heritage Archives.
12. Bob Funk interview.
13. Ibid.
14. Ibid.; www.med. umich.edu, the website of the University of Michigan School of Medicine.
15. Elnora Trim interview.
16. Interview with Joanne Marie Funk Benton, January 2, 2006, hereafter referred to as Joanne Benton interview, Heritage Archives.
17. Ibid.; Elnora Trim interview.
18. Ibid.
19. Joanne Benton interview.
20. Bob Funk interview.
21. Ibid.
22. Ibid.
23. Joanne Benton interview.
24. Ibid.
25. Bob Funk interview.
26. Joanne Benton interview.
27. Bob Funk interview.
28. Ibid.
29. Ibid.
30. Ibid.

three / Learning about Hard Work

1. Joanne Benton interview.
2. Bob Funk interview.
3. Ibid.
4. www.emchurch.
   lorg, the official website of the Evangelical Methodist Church.
5. Robert J. Morgan, *Then Sings My Soul: the World's Greatest Hymn Stories* (Nashville: Thomas Nelson Publishers, 2003), p. 297.
6. www.who2.com/ billygraham.
7. Bob Funk interview.
8. www.who2.com/ billygraham.
9. Bob Funk interview.
10. www.emchruch. org.
11. Bob Funk interview.
12. Bob Funk interview.
13. Ibid.
14. Ibid.
15. Joanne Benton interview.
16. Bob Funk interview.
17. Letter from Les Kinney to David Gillogly, December 28, 2005, Heritage Archives.
18. Letter from John Helm to David Gillogly, December 23, 2005, Heritage Archives.
19. Ibid.
20. Ibid.
21. Interview with Nedra Funk, January 10, 2006, hereafter referred to as Nedra Funk interview, Heritage Archives.
22. Bob Funk interview.
23. Ibid.
24. Ibid.
25. Ibid.

four / Off to College

1. Bob Funk interview.
2. www.historylink. org, "Seattle Seminary."
3. www.spu.edu, the official website of Seattle Pacific University.
4. Ibid.
5. Ibid.
6. Interview with Ernie Trim, September 30, 2006, hereafter referred to as Ernie Trim interview, Heritage Archives.
7. Ibid.
8. Bob Funk interview.
9. Ibid.
10. Ibid.
11. Ibid.
12. Ibid.
13. Nedra Funk interview.
14. Bob Funk interview.
15. Ibid.
16. Ibid.
17. Ibid.
18. Ibid.
19. Ibid.
20. Nedra Funk interview.

five / Edinburgh

1. Bob Funk interview.
2. Ibid.
3. Ibid.
4. Ibid.
5. Ibid.
6. www.en.wikipedia. org/University of Edinburgh.
7. Ibid.
8. Ibid.
9. www.ed.ac.uk, the official website of the University of Edinburgh.
10. Ibid.
11 Ibid.
12. Ibid.
13. Bob Funk interview.
14. Ibid.

15. Ibid.
16. Ibid.
17. Ibid.
18. Ibid.
19. Ibid.
20. Ibid.
21. Ibid.
22. Ibid.
23. Ibid.
24. Ibid.
25. Ibid.
26. Ibid.
27. Ibid.

six / A Cold Scottish Winter
1. Bob Funk interview.
2. Ibid.
3. Ibid.
4. Ibid.
5. Ibid.
6. Ibid.
7. Letter from Richard Trim to David Gillogly, February 14, 2006, Heritage Archives.
8. Bob Funk interview.
9. Ibid.
10. Ibid.
11. Ibid.
12. Ibid.

seven / A Change in Direction
1. Nedra Funk interview.
2. Ibid.
3. Ibid.

4. Ibid.
5. Joanne Benton interview.
6. Bob Funk interview.
7. Ibid.
8. Ibid.
9. Ibid.
10. Ibid.
11. Nedra Funk interview.
12. Bob Funk interview.
13. Nedra Funk interview.
14. Bob Funk interview.
15. Ibid.
16. Ibid.
17. Ibid.
18. Ibid.
19. Ibid.

eight / Inside Work
1. Bob Funk interview.
2. Ibid.
3. Ibid.
4. Ibid.
5. Lu Hollander, *Helping People Succeed, The Story of Express Personnel Services* (Oklahoma City: Express Services, Inc., 2003), hereafter referred to as *Helping People Succeed*, p. 12.

6. Ibid.
7. Bob Funk interview.
8. Ibid.
9. Ibid.
10. Ibid.
11. Ibid.
12. Ibid.
13. Ibid.
14. Interview with Ralph Palmen, December 15, 2005, hereafter referred to as Ralph Palmen interview.
15. Bob Funk interview.
16. *Helping People Succeed*, p. 14.
17. Bob Funk interview.
18. Nedra Funk interview.
19. Bob Funk interview.
20. Ibid.
21. Ibid.

nine / My Kind of Country
1. Bob Funk interview.
2. Ibid.
3. Ibid.
4. Interview with Esther Brindley, June 5, 2005, Heritage Archives.
5. Ibid.
6. Bob Funk interview.

7. Ralph Palmen interview.

8. Bob Funk interview.

9. Ibid.

10. www.piedmont.k12.ok.us, the official website of the Piedmont, Oklahoma School District.

11. Ibid.

12. Nedra Funk interview.

13. Bob Funk interview.

14. Letter from Mark and Sheryl Tasler to David Gillogoly, December 5, 2005, Heritage Archives, hereafter referred to as Mark and Sherly Tasler letter.

15. Ibid.

16. Ibid.

17. Ibid.

18. *Helping People Succeed*, p. 18.

19. Ibid., p. 20.

20. *The Daily Oklahoman,* July 29, 1973.

21. Nedra Funk interview.

22. *The Daily Oklahoman,* November 30, 1976.

23. *Piedmont-Surrey Gazette*, January 15, 1981.

24. Bob Funk interview.

25. Letter from R.B. Mathis to Dave Gillogly, December 30, 2005.

26. Bob Funk interview.

27. Ibid.

28. *Helping People Succeed*, p. 22.

29. Bob Funk interview.

30. Interview with Sandra VanZandt, February 28, 2007, hereafter referred to as Sandra VanZandt interview.

31. *Helping People Succeed*, p. 23

32. Interview with Carol Lane, February 28, 2007, hereafter referred to as Carol Lane interview.

33. Ibid.

34. *Helping People Succeed*, p. 24

35. Ibid.

36. Ibid.

37. Bob Funk interview.

38. Ibid.

39. Ibid.

40. Ibid.

41. *Helping People Succeed*, p. 28.

42. Bob Funk interview.

43. Ibid.

ten / Out of the Ashes

1. Ralph Palmen interview.

2. Bob Funk interview.

3. Purchase agreement of December 21, 1982, from the records of Express Services, Inc., Heritage Archives.

4. Ibid.

5. Ibid.; Bob Funk interview; financial statement of Apex Temporary Service, Heritage Archives.

6. Bob Funk interview.

7. *Helping People Succeed*, p. 35.

8. Ibid.

9. Ibid.

10 Ibid.

11. Ibid.

12. Ibid., p. 36.

13. Ibid.

14. Ibid.

15. Ibid.

16. Ibid., p. 37.

17. Ibid.

18. Ibid.

19. Ibid.

20. Ralph Palmen interview.
21. Ibid.
22. *Helping People Succeed,* p. 39.
23. Ibid., p. 38.
24. Ibid.
25. Ibid.
26. Interview with Nikki Sells, January 5, 2007, hereafter referred to as Nikki Sells interview.
27. *Helping People Succeed,* p. 40.
28. Nikki Sells interview.

eleven / Thriving Again
1. Bob Burke, *Good Guys Wear White Hats: The Life of George Nigh* (Oklahoma City: Oklahoma Heritage Association, 2000), p. 290.
2. Ibid.
3. Bob Funk interview.
4. Ibid.
5. Ibid.
6. Ibid.
7. *Helping People Succeed,* p. 47.
8. Ibid., p. 48.
9. Ibid., p. 52.
10. Ibid., p. 56.
11. Letter from Ralph Farrar to David Gillogly, January 10, 2006, Heritage Archives.
12. Ibid.
13. *Helping People Succeed,* p. 57.
14. Interview with Tom Gunderson, December 1, 2005, hereafter referred to as Tom Gunderson interview.
15. *Helping People Succeed,* p. 60.
16. Ibid.
17. Tom Gunderson interview.
18. Mark Tasler interview.
19. Ibid.
20. *The Daily Oklahoman,* September 23, 1988.
21. Ibid.
22. Ibid.
23. Interview with Linda Haneborg, February 7, 2007, hereafter referred to as Linda Haneborg interview.
24. Ibid.
25. Ibid.
26. *Helping People Succeed,* p. 102-103.
27. Bob Funk interview.
28. Interview with Scott Davis, February 12, 2006, Heritage Archives.
29. Letter from Harvey Homsey to David Gillogly, March 30, 2006, Heritage Archives.
30. Ibid.
31. www.recruitinglife.com, the official website of the National Association of Personnel Services.
32. www.hoovers.com/american-staffing-association.

twelve / Critical Times
1. Letter from David Gillogly to Bob Burke, September 28, 2006, Heritage Archives, hereafter referred to as David Gillogly letter.
2. Ibid.
3. Bob Funk interview.
4. Ibid.
5. Ibid.
6. Ibid.
7. Ibid.
8. Bob Funk interview.
9. Ibid.
10. Ibid.

11. David Gillogly letter.
12. Ibid.
13. Ibid.
14. Ibid.
15. Ibid.
16. Ibid.
17. Ibid.
18. Bob Funk interview.
19. Ibid.
20. Ibid.
21. Ibid.
22. Ibid.
23. Interview with Tom Richards, September 5, 2006.
24. Bob Funk interview.
25. David Gillogly letter, Bill Stoller interview.
26 Ibid.

thirteen / A Job for Every Person and a Person for Every Job
1. www.expresspersonnel.com
2. *Helping People Succeed*, p. 153.
3. Ibid.
4. Ibid.
5. Ibid., p. 158.
6. Ibid., p. 159.
7. Bob Funk interview.
8. Ibid.
9. Ibid.

10. Ibid.
11. Interview with Jim Britton, February 2, 2006, Heritage Archives.
12. Ibid.
13. Letter from Bonne McArthur and Elizabeth Shinn to David Gillogly, January 5, 2006, Heritage Archives.
14. Ibid.
15. Jim Britton interview.
16. Bob Funk interview.
17. Ibid.

fourteen / Strength for the Future
1. A collection of stories of franchise offices and consultants compiled by Sean Simpson, Express Archives.
2. Ibid.
3. Ibid.
4. Ibid.
5. Ibid.
6. Ibid.
7. Ibid.
8. Interview with Christine Menard, February 28, 2007, hereafter referred to as Christine Menard interview.
9. Ibid.
10. *Helping People*

Succeed, p. 227.
11. Ibid., p. 262.
12. Ibid., p. 312.
13. Bob Funk interview.
14. Ibid.
15. Letter from Sam Hammons to David Gillogly, February 22, 2006, Heritage Archives.
16. Ibid.
17. Ibid.
18. *Helping People Succeed*, p. 329.
19. Interview with Mary Fallin, September 29, 2006.
20. Interview with Bob Fellinger, September 11, 2006, hereafter referred to as Bob Fellinger interview.
21. Bob Funk interview.
22. Bob Fellinger interview.
23. Ibid.

fifteen / Bob—The Cowboy
1. www.ansi.okstate.edu, the official website of the National American Limousin Foundation.

2. Bob Funk inter-
view.
3. *The Daily
Oklahoman*,
September 3,
2003.
4. Ibid, February 15,
1998.
5. Ibid.
6. Ibid.
7. Bob Funk inter-
view.
8. www.express-
clydesdales.com
9. Ibid.
10. Ibid.
11. Ibid.
12. Hugh Jones, www.
okpetgazette.com
13. www.expressper-
sonnel.com
14. Agcomm.okstate.
edu
15. *The Daily
Oklahoman*,
February 26, 2006.
16. Bob Funk inter-
view.
17. www.en.wikipedia.
org/wiki/Dale_
Robertson
18. Letter from Dale
Robertson to
David Gillogly,
January 1, 2006,
Heritage Archives.
19. www.expressper-
sonnel.com
20. Letter from
Barbara Smith to
David Gillogly,

December 20,
2005.
21. Ibid.
22. Ibid.
23. Interview with
George Nigh ,
January 15, 2007,
hereafter referred
to as George Nigh
interview.

**sixteen / Pucks and
Lobs**
1. Bob Funk inter-
view.
2. Ibid.
3. Ibid.
4. Ibid.
5 Ibid.
6. *The Daily
Oklahoman*,
January 2, 2002.
7. Ibid.
8. Ibid.
9. Ibid., January 4,
2000.
10. Ibid., February 2,
2000.
11. Ibid., January 26,
2000.
12. Bob Funk inter-
view.
13. *The Daily
Oklahoman*, May
7, 2001.
14. Ibid., July 6, 2003.
15. Ibid., April 7,
2003.
16. Ibid., December
18, 2001.
17. Ibid.

18. Ibid.
19. Ibid., February 20,
2002.
20. Ibid.

**seventeen / Sultan of
Sports**
1. Quoting an
Associated Press
story, www.news-
star.com, July 4,
2003.
2. Ibid.
3. *The Daily
Oklahoman*, July 6,
2003.
4. Ibid.
5. Ibid.
6. Ibid., November
21, 2003.
7. Ibid.
8. Ibid., September
1, 2003.
9. Ibid., April 16,
2004.
10. Ibid.
11. Ibid., April 3,
2004.
12. Ibid., September
18, 2004.
13. Ibid., November
17, 2004.
14. Ibid., November
17, 2003.
15. Ibid., September
21, 2005.
16. Bob Funk inter-
view.
17. *The Daily
Oklahoman*,

November 14,
2003.
18. www.pbrnow.com,
the official website
of the Professional
Bull Riders, Inc.

**eighteen / Public
Service**
1. www.expressper-
sonnel.com/media-
center, the official
website of Express
Services, Inc.
2. Ibid.
3. Ibid.
4. Letter from
Cathy Keating to
David Gillogly,
December 15,
2005, Heritage
Archives, hereafter
referred to as
Cathy Keating
letter.
5. Letter from
Frank Keating to
David Gillogly,
December 15,
2005, Heritage
Archives, hereafter
referred to as
Frank Keating
letter.
6. Cathy Keating
letter.
7 Letter from Archie
Dunham to David
Gillogly, January
3, 2006, Heritage
Archives.

8. *The Daily
Oklahoman,*
January 6, 2002.
9. Letter from
Richard Burpee
to David Gillogly,
December 22,
2005, Heritage
Archives.
10. Ibid.
11. Ibid.
12. Ibid.
13. Ibid.
14. *The Daily
Oklahoman,*
February 8, 2004.
15. Bob Funk inter-
view.
16. Ibid.
17. *The Daily
Oklahoman,* June
6, 2005.
18. www.kc.frb.org,
the official website
of the Federal
Reserve Bank of
Kansas City.
19. Ibid.
20. Ibid.
21. Letter from
Thomas M.
Hoenig to David
Gillogly, January
5, 2006, Heritage
Archives.
22. *The Daily
Oklahoman,*
December 1,
2004.
23. Interview with Ed
Pease, November

30, 2005, Heritage
Archives.
24. Ibid.
25. Ibid.
26. www.expressper-
sonnel. com
27. Ibid.
28. Bob Funk inter-
view.
29. www.expressper-
sonnel.com
30. Linda Haneborg
interview.
31. Nedra Funk inter-
view.
32. Ibid.
33. www.skirvinhilton.
com

**nineteen / Giving
Hope**
1. Bob Funk inter-
view.
2. Interview with
Merv Hackney,
February 2, 2006,
Heritage Archives.
3. Ibid.
4. Interview with Bill
Stoller, February
28, 2007, Heritage
Archives.
5. Interview with
Cory Benton,
February 1, 2007.
6. Interview with
Paul Schulte,
February 4, 2006,
Heritage Archives.
7. Ibid.
8. Cathy Keating
letter.

9. Scott Davis inter-
   view.
10. George Nigh
    interview.
11. Letter from Sam
    Hammons to
    David Gillogly,
    February 22,

2006, Heritage
Archives.
12. Jerry Baird inter-
    view.
13. Ibid.
14. Linda Haneborg
    interview.
15. Nikki Sells inter-
    view.

The Next to the Last Chapter
1. *The Journal Record,*
   August 8, 2005.
2. Ibid.
3. Linda Haneborg
   interview.
4. Carol Lane inter-
   view.

INDEX

Acme International 133
Acme Personnel Services 84-85, 87-94, 103-108, 117-122, 133, 165
American Airlines 137-138
American Express 75
American Heart Association 232
American Staffing Association 142-143
ANCOR 161
Andex 112-114
Apex Temporary Service 118-119
Arden and Associates 158, 234-235
Arvanitis, Peter 196, 202
Asbury Theological Seminary 58
Ash, Neil 188
Atkinson, Art 109, 114, 122, 143, 155, 163
Atkinson, Gean 132, 139
Atmore Ranch 232

Bailey, Reid 90
Baillie, John 64
Baird, Jerry Magee 125, 127-128, 163, 241
Baptist Hospital 101
Barr, James 64
Base Realignment and Closure Commission 226
Bass Pro Shops 225
Baxter, Janet 142
Bench, Cindy 234
Benton, Cory 28, 234, 238, 245
Benton, Dave 28
Benton, Joanne Marie Funk 5, 24-48, 107, 121
Billy Graham Crusade 13
Black, Mary 5
Blair, Gordon 18, 84-85, 88-89, 93, 96, 114, 178
Blair, Jeanne 178
Bontrager, David 183
Boren, David 147
Boutwell, Andi 234

Boy Scouts of America 232
Branch, Rod 202
Brannon, Ruby 99, 113
Bridges, Bailey Ruth 158, 236
Bridges, Bowen James 158, 236, 242
Bridges, Christopher "Chris" 158, 231
Bridges, Julie Funk 97, 107, 109, 115, 130, 158, 191, 232-233
Brindley Personnel 100
Brindley, Esther 99-101
British Airways 62
Britton, Jim 165-166
Brock, John 228
Brooks, John 200
Burpee, Richard 224-225
Burton, Joe 202
Bush, George W. 242
Butler, Rod 203

Callahan, Jarold 181
Camp, Pat 170

Camp, Randall 170
Campbell, Corbin 203
Campbell, Gini Moore 5
Carnation Dairy 16
Carnation, WA 16-17
Central Hockey League 198-206
Checkpoint Charlie 75
Chen, Horn 198-200
Cherry Valley Grade School 32, 34-35, 79
Chesapeake Energy 193
Chicago, Milwaukee, and St. Paul Railroad 15
Children's Miracle Network 188, 190, 233
Chisholm Trail 193
Church of the Nativity 68
City National Bank 99
Clark, Eddie 93
CNA Insurance Company 149-150
ConocoPhillips 224
Continental Basketball Association 198
Cornett, Mick 218
Corrigan, Chris 124, 141
Country Treasures 105
Cowley, Abraham 237
Cox Business Services Convention Center 207, 218
Craig, Jeri 135-137
Crawford House Hotel 192

Dabney, Eric 5
Dallas Stars 201
Dand, Viola 91
Davis Cup 206-210
Davis, George 5
Davis, Joe 57, 83
Davis, Marcia 5
Davis, Scott 142, 239
Davison, Robin 5
Deaconess Hospital 105
Dean, James 101
Deck, Glenn 201-202
Demeray, Don 62
DeVos, Dan 201
Douglas, Michelle 5
Doyle, Sir Athur Conan 64
Drury, Dean 136
Dun & Bradstreet 84-85
Dunham, Archie W. 224
Duvall Evangelical Methodist Church 11-13, 31-33, 37-38, 41-42, 68
Duvall, Francis 15
Duvall, James 15
Dynasty 194

Eaton, Doug 178
Edinburgh Castle 64
Edinburgh, Scotland 51-67
Egan, Kathy 125
Egan, Michael 124-125
Eidenmuller, Hank 133
Emerson, Ralph Waldo 236

Ernst & Young 238
Evangelical Methodist Church 38, 41
Exchange 139
Express Advisory Council 195
Express Business Solutions 176
Express Ranches 181-186
Express Ranches Progressive Junior Scholarship Program 193
Express Sports 206-208, 210
Express Temporary Help Service, Inc. 120, 122-123
Expressions 139, 156
Extra 139

Fairchild, Cindy 114, 127, 132, 142
Fallin, Mary 175
Falls Creek Baptist Youth Camp 224
Fangman, Paul 136
Farrar, Cheri 5
Farrar, Ralph 134-135
Federal Reserve Bank of Kansas City 228-231
Federal Reserve System 228-231
Federal Trade Commission 135
Fellinger, Bob 153, 175-176
Fidelity National Bank 101, 105
First City Bank 151

Ford Center 201, 218
Fox, George 7
Framme, Cyndi 172
Franco, Francisco 73
Frazier, Hugh 65-67, 69
Friesen, Bob 81
Frist, Bill 242
Funk, Allen Roy 17-39, 81, 121, 128-129
Funk, Dorothy Ellen Herman 17-39, 72, 74-77, 81
Funk, Mariann 22, 24
Funk, Nedra Pitcher 48-49, 55-59, 69-70, 77, 79-85, 96-97, 100-111, 130, 135, 162, 178, 191, 197, 234-235, 244
Funk, Pearl Addleman 16-19, 82
Funk, Robert Allen "Bob" childhood 11-51, college 53-77, Acme Personnel 79-95, Express Personnel 125-179, ranching 181-195, sports ownership 197-219, public service 221-236
Funk, Robert Allen "Bobby", Jr. 105, 109, 129-130, 159, 191, 210
Funk, William Allen 17

Future Farmers of America 42, 47-48, 53

Gaylord Entertainment Company 213
Gillogly, David 132, 140, 147-149, 152, 168, 172, 200, 216
Gore, Amanda 173
Graham, Billy 10-13, 38, 41, 242
Granada Royale Hotel 129
Gray, Carol 110, 124, 127-128
Gray, Jim 110, 119-120, 122-127, 133-134, 147, 151
Great Depression 17
Greenspan, Alan 229-230
Gresham, Linda 162
Gresham, Loren 162
Grimes, H.I. 182
Gunderson, Dan 159
Gunderson, Tom 89, 93, 104, 114, 124-125, 127, 135, 137, 159, 163, 168

Hackney, Merv 238
Haglind, Midrael 154
Hamblen, J.H. 38
Hamblen, Stuart 38
Hammons, Sam 174-175, 239
Haneborg, Linda 5, 132, 139-141, 163, 168, 234, 241, 245-246

Hanisch Farm 49
Hanisch, Adolph 48-49, 51, 59, 81, 83-84
Hanisch, Anna Pauline 18
Hanish, Frank Emil 19
Hansen, Paul 217
Hard Rock Café 234
Hargis, Burns 226
Harrington, Bernie 157
Harry, Billie 5
Hayer, Melissa 5
Haymaker, Willis Graham 38
Helm, John 45-46
Henkle, Dellamae 125
Henry, Brad 228
Herman, Albert 19, 21
Herman, Amelia 19
Herman, Art 19, 21
Herman, Carol 26
Herman, Emma Marie 17-19
Herman, Gail 26
Herman, Julius Carl 17
Herman, Mae 19
Herman, Nora 26
Herman, Ruth 26
Herman, Susie 26, 43
Hoening, Thomas M. 230-231
Hollander, Lu 175
Holy Land 66-68
Homsey, Harvey 142
Humphreys, Kirk 198, 200, 201

IGA Tennis Classic 207

Inside Track 139
International
 Franchising
 Association 221
International Hockey
 League 198-199
International
 Leadership
 Conference 174,
 179

J.J. Starbuck 194
John the Baptist 69
Johnson Controls
 Company 225
Johnson, Lynne 171
Jordan River 69

**Kansas City Blades
 198, 201**
Keating, Cathy 222,
 239
Keating, Frank 174,
 209, 222
Kelley, Doug 170
Kelley, Kathy 170
Kelly Girl 94-96
Kelly Labor 94-96
Kelly Services 94-96
Kidwell, Ginny 118
King James VI 63
King, William Rufus
 15-16
Kinney, Les 45-46
Kjack, Dale 93, 119,
 122
Kuker, Dave 163

**Lane, Carol 111, 127,
 139, 163, 246**
Larson, Gordon 93,
 114
Lemons, Abe 217
Little, Dean 96

Long, E.H. 101
Loria, Jeffrey 213
Lower Carnation, WA
 18
Lund, Brad 197-200,
 106-207, 210-211,
 215
Lynn, Linda 5

Mackie, Hugh 64-65
Mackintosh, H.R. 64
Macklanburg-Duncan
 100
Magee Enterprises,
 Inc. 124
Magee, Jerry 113
Magee, Paul 125
Manning, MaryAnn
 Spencer 155
Martin, Jim 106
Martin, Laura 106
Mathis, R.B. 106-107
McArthur, Bonne 165
McCormick, Bill 31
McDonald, Emma
 188
Menard, Christine 171
Michalson, Ethel 24
Minshull, Josh 192
Mitchell, Dale 132,
 134, 147
Monroe High Schol
 42, 44
Monroe, WA 42, 44
Montgomery, Lois
 127-128
Mullanix, Susan
 109-110, 118, 122,
 124, 127-128
Muse, Fred 178
MyIne's Court 63
Myriad Convention
 Center 199, 226

**National Association
 of Personnel
 Services 142**
National Association
 of Temporary
 Services 143
National Basketball
 Association
 217-219
National Clydesdales
 Show 191
National Cowboy and
 Western Heritage
 Museum 193
National Hockey
 League 197, 217
Navarre, Corey
 218-219
Neill, Debbie 5
New College 63
New College Seminary
 58
New Orleans Hornets
 218
Newberry, Jody 218-
 219
Nicklin, Brant 202
Nigh, George 131,
 195, 239-240
North American
 Limousin
 Foundation 193
Novikova, Elna 161
Nurman, Lars 154

**Ogilvie, Lloyd John
 7-8**
Oklahoma Baptist
 University 159,
 221-222
Oklahoma Baseball
 Club, LLC 216

Oklahoma Christian University of Science and Arts 222
Oklahoma City Blazers 196-206
Oklahoma City Cavalry 198
Oklahoma City Chamber of Commerce 224-224
Oklahoma City University 217
Oklahoma Limousin Breeders Association 193
Oklahoma Personnel Service, Inc. 118
Oklahoma RedHawks 213-217
Oklahoma State Chamber of Commerce 228
Oklahoma State Insurance Fund 147
Oklahoma State University 193-194, 231
Oklahoma Youth Expo 193-194
Olsten Personnel 112
Owens, David R. 105
Oxford University 66

Pacific Coast League 213-217
Pacific Ocean 15
Palmen, Darlys 120, 125
Palmen, Ralph 90-91, 100-101, 117, 120, 124-125, 127-128
Pease, Ed 232
Penfold, Matthew 178
Penn, William 7
Peppin, Ed 126
Peterson, Ed 41-42
Peterson, Nils B. 54
Phillips Pavilion 222
Phillips, Mary 5
Phillips, Waite 232
Philmont Ranch 232
Pickens, Boone 231
Piedmont Board of Education 104-106
Piedmont High School 105, 134
Piedmont-Surrey Gazette 106
Pierce, Franklin 16
Pinson, Nell 124
Pitcher, Francis 39-41, 57-58, 80-84
Pitcher, Kay 81
Pitcher, Ruth 49
Prince Philip 240
Prix de West Society 193
Professional Bull Riders, Inc. 218
Project Lupesi 233-234
Pruitt, Scott 213-217
Puget Sound 15

Quad Graphics Printing Company 225
Queen Anne Hill 54

Radia, Chandu 137
Ray Miran Cup 202

Reiff, David L. 88-91, 93
Reiff, Steve 117-120, 122
Reiff, William "Bill" 89-92, 95-96, 99-102, 113-115, 117-119
Renberg, Oscar 38
Rice, Peyton 124-125
Richards, Tom 132, 151-153, 163
Richardson, Leroy 238
Rickey, Branch 216
Ripkin, Cal, Jr. 173
Robertson, Dale 194
Roby, Richard 132, 136, 139
Rockaway Camp 79
Roddick, Andy 207
Rohde, John 202
Roney, Ward 22
Royal Mile 63

Sales and Marketing Executives International Hall of Fame 221
Sampras, Pete 207
Samuel Roberts Noble Foundation 193
Sasser, Linda 143
Sauter, Doug 192, 197, 199, 206, 215
Sav-Go 105
SBC Bricktown Ballpark 213-217
Schuller, Robert 173
Schulte, Paul 238
Schwarzkopf, Norman 230

Scofield, Jerry 124,
  241
Scott, Sir Walter 64
Seattle Pacific College
  (Seattle Pacific
  University) 53-59,
  62, 76, 81-85, 177,
  221
Seattle Seminary 53
Seles, Monica 207
Sells, Nikki 127-129,
  241
Shakespeare, William
  237
Shea, George Beverly
  11
Shinn, Elizabeth 165
Silver Springs Crossing
  225
Skirvin Hotel 99, 235
Smith, Barbara 195
Snohomisy County
  WA 42
Snoqualmie River
  15-17
Snoqualmie Valley
  16-17, 26, 35
Sonic Industries 135
Southern Nazarene
  University 162, 221
St. Louis-El Reno-
  Western Railroad
  101
Steiger, Ann 99
Stevenson, Robert
  Louis 64
Stewart, James 58, 64
Stoller, William H.
  "Bill" 103-104,
  110, 119-120,
  122-129, 133-134,

137, 144, 147, 168,
  230, 240, 246
Strum, Jody 28
Stuart, Elbridge Amos
  16

Taft Stadium 11, 38
Tales of Wells Fargo 194
Tasler, Mark 103, 124,
  133, 141, 160, 241
Tasler, Sheryl 103
Thacker, Jeremy 169
The Daily Oklahoman
  104, 123, 201, 217,
  226
Times Square Hotel
  75-76
Tinker Air Force Base
  225-226
Tito, Marshall 67
Tolt, WA 16-17
Topliff, Nancy 128
Torrance, T.E. 64
Tramel, Berry
  206-207, 215
Trim, Elnora 24, 80
Trim, Ernie 54
Trim, Richard "Dick"
  24, 42, 73-75, 81
Tulsa Oilers 219

*U.S. News and World
  Report* 132
United States Tennis
  Association 207
University of Central
  Oklahoma 158
University of
  Edinburgh 58,
  60-66, 70-72
University of Kentucky
  213

University of London
  66
University of Puget
  Sound 18
University of Tulsa
  213
University of
  Washington 89
USS *President
  Cleveland* 18

**Van Treeck, Dorothy
  110**
Vance Building 90
VanZant, Sandra 109,
  111, 127, 142-143
Village Inn Pancake
  House 195

Wagner, Ken 216
Wainscott, Alta 37
Wainscott, Vida 37,
  43
Walesa, Lech 220
Washington Natural
  Gas Company 79,
  89, 95
Watson, C. Hoyt 54
Watts, J.C. 217
Welch, Sandi 5
Weldon, Terri 28, 106,
  127, 172
Whitefield, Justin 194
Williams, Bern 236
Williams, Venus 207
Wilson, Talmadge 82
Wolff, Vonda 143
World War II 88, 100,
  183

**Zettlemoyer, Debbie
  192**